WALKING ON THE
ISLE OF ARRAN

Little waterfalls rumble downhill with Beinn Nuis seen beyond (Walk 39)

WALKING ON THE
ISLE OF ARRAN

by
Paddy Dillon

CICERONE PRESS
MILNTHORPE, CUMBRIA

© P. Dillon 1998
ISBN 1 85284 269 5
A catalogue record for this book is available from the British Library.

Front Cover: Looking to Cir Mhor and Goat Fell from
Caisteal Abhail's summit. (Walk 24)

CONTENTS

ISLE OF ARRAN

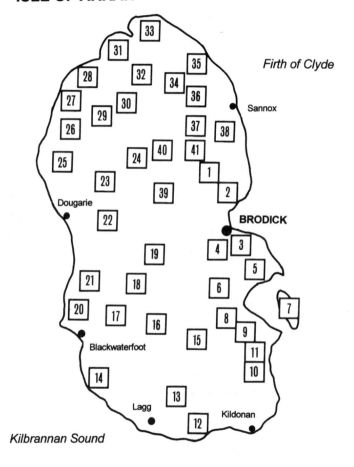

Firth of Clyde

Sannox

Dougarie

BRODICK

Blackwaterfoot

Lagg

Kildonan

Kilbrannan Sound

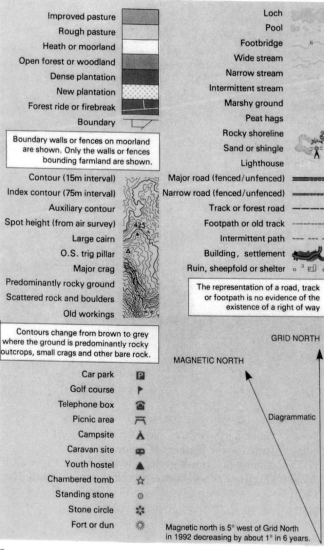

Improved pasture
Rough pasture
Heath or moorland
Open forest or woodland
Dense plantation
New plantation
Forest ride or firebreak
Boundary

Boundary walls or fences on moorland
are shown. Only the walls or fences
bounding farmland are shown.

Contour (15m interval)
Index contour (75m interval)
Auxiliary contour
Spot height (from air survey)
Large cairn
O.S. trig pillar
Major crag
Predominantly rocky ground
Scattered rock and boulders
Old workings

Contours change from brown to grey
where the ground is predominantly rocky
outcrops, small crags and other bare rock.

Car park
Golf course
Telephone box
Picnic area
Campsite
Caravan site
Youth hostel
Chambered tomb
Standing stone
Stone circle
Fort or dun

Loch
Pool
Footbridge
Wide stream
Narrow stream
Intermittent stream
Marshy ground
Peat hags
Rocky shoreline
Sand or shingle
Lighthouse
Major road (fenced/unfenced)
Narrow road (fenced/unfenced)
Track or forest road
Footpath or old track
Intermittent path
Building, settlement
Ruin, sheepfold or shelter

The representation of a road, track
or footpath is no evidence of the
existence of a right of way

GRID NORTH

MAGNETIC NORTH

Diagrammatic

Magnetic north is 5° west of Grid North
in 1992 decreasing by about 1° in 6 years.

INTRODUCTION

The Isle of Arran rises proudly from the Firth of Clyde between Ayrshire and Kintyre. Its mountainous form dominates the open waters of the Clyde and its jagged peaks present a challenge to walkers. People first came to the island some 5500 years ago, though its history is but dimly recorded. Tourism has been important for only the past century. The Isle of Arran has much to offer the visitor and is often described as "Scotland in Miniature". Roads are very few, but opportunities to explore the island on foot are many and varied. This guidebook offers a selection of forty-one day walks all over the island.

A GEOLOGY CLASSROOM
The Isle of Arran is one of the most varied geological areas in the British Isles. A wag once noted that while some people write to *The Times* when they hear the first cuckoo of spring, others write to the *Arran Banner* when they hear the chipping of the first geologist of spring! The island is like a huge geological classroom and groups of students will often be seen in careful study.

James Hutton, the redoubtable scientist from Edinburgh, visited the Isle of Arran in August 1787. He was the first person to identify an "unconformity" - where rocks of widely differing ages rest together at different angles. In fact, an unconformity on the coast north of Lochranza is known to this day as Hutton's Unconformity. Hutton expounded a "Theory of the Earth" in which mountains were continually being uplifted and eroded, although few took the great man seriously. Geologists of Hutton's day were divided into the "Vulcanists" and "Neptunists" according to whether they believed rocks were formed by volcanic action or by deposition as sediments. Hutton's theory embraced both concepts and today he is widely regarded as the "Father of Geology".

While the study of Arran's geology is very much a specialist subject, there are a few notes which are worth bearing in mind. The oldest rocks on Arran occur on the northern half of the island. Cambrian strata, originally marine muds and sands, have been altered by tremendous heat and pressure into slates and sparkling schists, often streaked with veins of white quartz. In a semi-circle around this base rock are Devonian strata, composed originally of desert sand dunes, and revealed in an arc from Sannox to Dougarie. A more disjointed arc of Carboniferous strata stretches from Lochranza to Sannox and from Corrie to the String Road. These include limestones, sandstones and workable coal measures, all formed in shallow seas or on a swampy delta. Permian strata again indicate desert conditions, with sand dunes, and these sandstones take up much of central and southern parts of Arran. Triassic strata stretch across the southernmost part of the island, from Blackwaterfoot to Kildonan, and are composed of muds and sands laid down in a lake or delta system.

Into this basic succession of strata were intruded masses of molten rock under great heat and pressure, which had the effect of baking the surrounding strata and altering their mineral structures and appearance. The granite peaks of northern Arran are formed from a massive intrusive boss of granite. Around southern Arran, molten rock was squeezed into bedding planes and joints to create resistant sills and dykes. Some splendid igneous dykes stand as obvious walls of rock all around the southern coast.

On a geological timescale, the final act in the shaping of Arran occurred during the Ice Age. The Isle of Arran was prominent enough to support its own ice cap, grinding corries and "U" shaped valleys quite independent of the massive highland glaciers scouring out the troughs of the Clyde and Kilbrannan Sound. The power of the ice inexorably grinding into the rocky mountains was one thing, but the weight of the ice was also important. As the Ice Age drew to a close, meltwater raised the sea levels, but as the weight of the ice was lifted from the earth's crust, there was a corresponding uplift of part of the surface. This can be noted all around Arran, as well as all around the Scottish coast, where cobbly raised beaches, marooned sea stacks and marine caves some distance from the sea can be identified.

Walkers with a special interest in geology should use a specific field guide to the geology of the island, such as *Macgregor's Excursion Guide to the Geology of Arran*, edited and revised by J.G. MacDonald and A. Herriot, published by the Geological Society of Glasgow.

A TURBULENT HISTORY

The first people to have approached Arran would have found a forested island with only the highest peaks protruding above the tree canopy. Evidence of this former forest can be seen in some peat bogs, where trunks, branches and root systems of trees have been preserved. Neolithic hunters and farmers left no discernible traces of their settlements, but they did leave massive chambered burial cairns, most notably around the southern half of the island. Bronze Age communities left traces of hut circles, stone circles and smaller burial cairns. The best examples are found around Machrie Moor and Blackwaterfoot. The remains point to settled, well-organised communities. The Iron Age is characterised by the construction of small, fortified hill forts, suggesting a measure of insecurity or strife, and again these are to be found mainly around the southern half of the island. The early language forms are unknown, with no

Rock painting on Holy Isle by Tibetan artist Dekyi Wangmo

written or spoken elements surviving. The Gaelic language of the later Celtic peoples, however, has survived in the Western Isles, although it is not commonly spoken or written on Arran today.

St. Ninian is credited with bringing Christianity into Scotland from his base at Whithorn. He and other missionaries would have sailed around the coastline, visiting small communities and hopping from island to island. Ninian is known to have visited Bute and Sanda, both near Arran, and he died in the year 424. The most notable saint on Arran was St. Las, born in the year 566, who lived as a hermit in a cave on Holy Isle and later became the Abbot of Leithglinn in Ireland. He died in the year 639. King's Cave near Blackwaterfoot is thought to have been occupied by early missionaries on inter-island expeditions. The island kingdom was known as Dalriada and was a great Gaelic stronghold.

Viking raiding parties hit Iona in the year 759, and later harrassed the Isle of Arran and surrounding island and coastal areas. Later waves of settlers left traces of farmsteads and Norse placenames - including Goat Fell. Arran became, along with neighbouring territories, very much a property of the Norsemen. The great Somerled, progenitor of the great clans MacDonald and Ranald, led a force against the Norse in 1156 and became ruler of old Dalriada, although the islands were still nominally under Norse sovereignty. The emergence of Scotland as an independent state was enhanced following the defeat of the Norsemen at the Battle of Largs, opposite Arran, in 1263. When Norway sold the islands to Scotland in 1266 Alexander III granted Arran to Walter Stewart. The early history of Scotland, and more especially of Arran, is but scantily recorded. Much energy and strife accompanied Robert the Bruce's bitter campaign to secure the Scottish throne, culminating in the Battle of Bannockburn in 1314. For centuries Scottish history was wrought in terms of bitter border disputes with England. The islands largely continued to exist as Gaelic strongholds with a definable culture.

What is known of Arran's history is that many farmsteads were granted by the Scottish kings, who claimed a rent on them. The few stout castles on the island were at some time controlled by the Stewarts before coming into the hands of the Hamiltons. The first Marquis of Hamilton was appointed to administer peace and justice on Arran in 1609. The name Hamilton is strongly associated with the later development of the island. A succession of them held the title of Dukes of Hamilton, Brandon and Chatelherault, with Brodick Castle as their chief base. The population seems to have increased to the point where many were living in poor clachans (farming settlements), heralding a time of tremendous social changes. Much has been written about the Arran Clearances, when the old system of land tenancy was completely changed and much of the population was either re-settled in purpose-built cottages, or emigrated to the New World; most notably Canada. Immediately following these drastic changes, tourism began to develop and has continued apace, with walking and the enjoyment of the outdoors being a prime pursuit. The Arran Heritage Centre at Brodick offers an insight into the last century of life on the Isle of Arran - a century which has at least been fairly well documented!

For further details of Arran's history, consider reading *Exploring Arran's Past*, by Horace Fairhurst, published by Kilbrannan Publishing.

LAND OWNERSHIP & ACCESS

It is possible to define three main areas of land ownership on the Isle of Arran. The Arran Estate comprises much of northern Arran, including many high mountains and bleak, remote wilderness moorland areas. The estate is practically enclosed by a continuous tall deer fence, although this is not to be taken as an exact boundary. However, within the estate deer are given free range and are prevented from encroaching on neighbouring farms or forestry properties, where they could cause great damage. Deer stalking takes place on some parts of the estate at certain times and notices are usually displayed requesting walkers to stick to clearly defined paths. At other times, there seems to be no great objection to walkers unobtrusively heading off in almost any direction.

Much of southern Arran is owned by the Forestry Commission, which exists primarily to ensure that there are always rotating stocks of timber. While the forests may seem dark, dingy and unattractive to many walkers, there is at least a policy of allowing virtual free access, except at times when harvesting operations constitute a hazard. Not all the land owned by the Forestry Commission has been planted with trees. Some areas are not suitable for planting, including some wet moorland areas and steep mountainsides, where good quality walking can still be enjoyed.

The National Trust for Scotland owns a sizeable parcel of land which includes, and extends beyond, Glen Rosa, Goat Fell and the surrounding mountains. The land is managed both for conservation and recreation. Generally, walkers are free to head in any direction they choose, and this tends to be the busiest mountain area on the island. The proximity of Brodick and the main ferry service ensures that this will remain the busiest walking area.

The fringe of the Isle of Arran is mostly occupied by farms and villages. Access to farmlands may be quite limited in some areas, and walkers should not cross fields and other enclosures by climbing over walls and fences. Use only regular paths and tracks when negotiating farmland, and as far as possible stick to routes which are already in regular use. There is a relatively high degree of access on the Isle of Arran, but it is important that walkers and other visitors respect the rights of landowners and tenants, whose livelihood is vested in the land.

The Arran Deer Management Group has placed the following notice at various points around northern Arran:

Walkers are welcome. The members of this Deer Management Group recognise the tradition of free access to the hill. The Deer Management Group is responsible for the management and conservation of the land, in particular the management of red deer. The main deer management aims are:

* to maintain a healthy red deer herd in balance with the natural habitat.

* to maintain local employment and through this to support the rural community and local businesses.

* to conserve the natural qualities of the land including its wildlife.

The National Trust for Scotland is also a member of this Deer Management Group. Its policies ensure that the public access is unaffected when culling/stalking takes place. Please help the privately owned stalking estates to achieve these aims, particularly during the main stag stalking season from mid-August to mid-October, by:

> * avoiding areas where stalking is taking place.

> * seeking information in advance so that you can plan your visit to avoid disturbance to stalking.

> * following any local guidance on the day.

All members of this Deer Management Group will be pleased to recommend walking routes which will enable you to enjoy the area.

Information on stalking in Arran is available through the Hillphone answering service, tel: 01770 302363, whose message is updated daily. Thank you.

FLORA & FAUNA

Arran is an island, so on the way there keep a look out for occasional small whales or dolphins which might be seen from the ferry, and note that seals may be basking on rocky parts of the shore all around the island. There are no foxes or stoats; there are red squirrels, but no greys. Otters are coming under pressure from feral mink in the watercourses. Some 2000 red deer thrive on northern Arran and are selectively stalked and culled as they have no natural predators. Brown hares are often noted on southern Arran. Reptiles are represented by adders, lizards and slow worms, which can all be noted basking in the open on sunny days. There are plenty of frogs in places, as well as salmon and trout. Dainty dragonflies and butterflies swell the summer air, but there are also hordes of midges best defeated by strong sun, a stiff sea breeze, or copious applications of insect repellent!

Bird life is dominated by golden eagles, hawks and ravens in the mountain environment. Owls include barn owl, tawny owl, long and short-eared owl. The varied coastline supports eider, shag, cormorants, mallard, shelduck, mergansers, redshank, ringed plover, turnstone, oystercatcher, wigeon, goldeneye and many types of gull. Gannets have a colony on Ailsa Craig and may be observed diving spectacularly for fish near Arran, while fulmars nest all around the cliffs. Herons can be noted along many watercourses, as well as beside the sea, and there are plenty of forest and meadow species to be noted.

There is a specific field guide to the bird life of the island and keen ornithologists may like to read *Birds of Arran* by John Rhead & Philip Snow, published by Saker Press. There is also a periodical called *The Arran Bird Report*, published by the Arran Natural History Society.

The flora of Arran is another specialist study. The original canopy forest is now reduced to a few ancient stands of oak, ash, rowan or hazel. These areas will often be home to wood sorrel and bluebells. Notable trees include the rare Arran Service trees in Gleann Diomhan. Forest species include spruce, larch, pines and firs. There are some introduced species which have become nuisances, such as rhododendron and Himalayan balsam. There are also some small, specialised trees to be found in even the most barren mountain areas; generally dwarf willow and creeping juniper.

The range of habitat types gives a roothold to some 500 species of flowering plants. A great variety of specialist plants are to be found on the raised beaches and sea cliffs, but there are far too many to list here. Lowland wetlands are often bright with wild iris; slopes may be dominated by invasive bracken; while moorland areas may be flushed purple with heather. Bilberry, bog myrtle and bog asphodel are common on the boggy uplands. The mountain environment supports plants such as alpine lady's mantle, alpine sawwort, starry saxifrage, mossy saxifrage and mountain sorrel. Some boggy areas feature insectivorous butterwort and sundew. Foxgloves, ragwort and rosebay willowherb are markers of disturbed ground, and hence tend to flourish alongside forest tracks and roads. Tucked away in many dark and damp crevices are an abundance of ferns, for which Arran is notable. Like the coastal plants, ferns are a specialist study.

There is a specific field guide to the flora of Arran which interested botanists may find useful: *Arran's Flora* by Tony Church & Tony Smith, published by the Arran Natural History Society. *The Arran Naturalist* is a periodical also published by the Society.

ACCOMMODATION ON ARRAN

There is a wide range of accommodation on the Isle of Arran, but be warned in advance that it becomes fully booked at peak periods. Either book a bed well in advance, or choose to walk off-season. At the lower level there are a mere handful of campsites and wild camping is discouraged - especially in Glen Rosa. There is a bunkhouse at Corrie and youth hostels at Whiting Bay and Lochranza. Bed and breakfast establishments are found all the way around the island, notably in the villages, but also on some of the farms. Large hotels are located in Brodick, Lamlash, Whiting Bay and Blackwaterfoot, though there are small hotels in some of the other villages. Self-catering houses and cottages are abundant. For food and drink, there are plenty of cafes and restaurants, including pub grub and, unusually, little tearooms attached to some of the golf courses willingly cater to the general public.

Full details of the island's facilities can be obtained from the Tourist Information Centre. There is an accommodation list too, as well as an accommodation booking service.

FAMILIARISATION WITH ARRAN

Motorists arriving at Brodick by ferry from Ardrossan are confronted by a sign offering only three directions: North, South and West. East is the ferry back to the mainland! There is one main road encircling the Isle of Arran, the A841, which links practically all of the villages on the island. In a clockwise order these include: Brodick, Lamlash, Whiting Bay, Kildonan, Kilmory, Sliddery, Blackwaterfoot, Machrie, Pirnmill, Catacol, Lochranza, Sannox, Corrie and so back to Brodick. There are two roads running across the island. The String, or the B880, runs from Brodick to Blackwaterfoot via Shiskine, although there is a minor road spur to Machrie. The Ross is a minor road running from Lamlash to a point near Sliddery. All the roads are equipped with distinctive red sandstone milestones, each inscribed with a number. Motorists have the option, in the summer months, of reaching the Isle of Arran via the Claonaig ferry from Kintyre which docks at the slipway at Lochranza.

While cars can be brought onto the island, it is an extra expense when the road use is so limited. There is a reasonably good bus service operated by Stagecoach Western Scottish, which often ties in well with many of the walks. All services on the island, including Post Bus services and ferries, with some mainland connections too, are contained in timetable booklets published for the summer and winter seasons. Note especially the variations during school holidays

Post Bus services augment those of the regular bus services

and Sundays. In the interests of "green" pursuits, walkers may wish to patronise these services. All the walks in this guidebook, for instance, were completed relying entirely on the public transport network.

THE WALKS

The walks in this guidebook include a couple of easy, waymarked forest trails, as well as a dozen or so moderate glen or hill walks. The rest require more effort to complete, heading for the higher mountains and sometimes involving a bit of hands-on scrambling. The routes are sometimes along roads or clear forest tracks, sometimes along hill tracks or paths, or even crossing pathless slopes and traversing rocky mountain ridges. The more off the beaten track the walker wanders, the more care needs to be exercised. Bouldery slopes or tussocky moorlands are indicated in advance; places where an ankle is easily turned. Steep, rocky scrambles requiring the use of hands are also noted, so that more cautious walkers can decide whether or not to proceed. All forty-one of the walks have been chosen to show off the rich variety of landscape types on the Isle of Arran. They seek secluded spots, or aim for the heights, indulging in wide-ranging views, or searching for some heritage detail.

Longer routes can be pieced together using portions of the route descriptions. Many of the walks in this guide overlap, or have sections in common, so that it is easy to extend or shorten many of the routes. Some walks stand in isolation, having no easy or quality links with other walks.

THE MAPS

The maps used throughout this guidebook are extracted from Harveys Walkers Maps of Arran North and Arran South. Originally, there was a single map published by Harveys for the Karrimor Mountain Marathon, which was held on the Isle of Arran in 1980. There are now two maps and two scales available - 1:40,000 and 1:25,000 - all regularly updated. The maps are remarkable in the way they show the features of the landscape with great clarity. Accurate contouring changes from brown to grey when the ground becomes predominantly rocky. Cliffs and screes are shown, as well as cairns, boggy ground and peat hags. Paths and tracks are noted where they are clear enough to be followed, with forest tracks shown where they are present. Forests and enclosed farmland are easily distinguished from open mountain and moorland, with the lines of some prominent upland walls or fences also shown. While the maps in this guidebook are shown in monochrome, Harveys maps are in full colour and are printed on waterproof paper, as well as being supplied with a protective plastic sleeve. Harveys Maps, 12-16 Main Street, Doune, Perthshire FK16 6BJ. Telephone: (01786) 841202.

The relevant Ordnance Survey maps covering the Isle of Arran are: Landranger sheet 69 at a scale of 1:50,000 and Outdoor Leisure sheet 37 at a scale of 1:25,000.

TOURIST INFORMATION

The Tourist Information Centre for the Isle of Arran is located at the ferry terminal in Brodick. The office can handle requests about accommodation, public transport and other services. Beds can be booked in advance, and it is possible to buy specific maps and field guides covering all aspects of the island. Contact: Isle of Arran Tourist Board, Tourist Information Centre, Brodick, Isle of Arran KA27 8AU. Telephone: (01770) 302140.

WALK 1
Goat Fell & Brodick

There are some walkers who step off the Caledonian MacBrayne ferry at Brodick and head straight away in the direction of Goat Fell, hoping to climb to its summit and return in time to leave the island. It's a grand day out for those who have the energy to complete the ascent between ferries, and this route description is offered just for them. Others may enjoy Goat Fell by a variety of other routes and tackle the ascent with less urgency. Basically, the route leads along the main road from Brodick, cutting a corner near the Arran Heritage Museum, then starting the ascent in earnest above the Arran Craft Centre at Clachan. The route is a combination of roads, tracks and a rugged, well-worn path. It is quite likely that other walkers will be met on the way there and back as this is the most popular way up and down Goat Fell. The initial road-walk could be cut out by catching a bus to the Arran Craft Centre from Brodick. Walkers intending to catch a bus back to link with the ferry should carry up-to-date timetables.

The Route

Distance:	10$^{1}/_{2}$ miles (17km)
Start:	Ferry Terminal, Brodick, grid ref 022358.
Terrain:	Roads, forest tracks, rugged moorland and mountain paths. Some of the upper parts are loose and stony.

Buses generally meet the ferry as it arrives at Brodick Pier. Some walkers may wish to hop onto the bus which goes around the northern half of the Isle of Arran, using it to reach the Arran Craft Centre near Brodick Castle. Those who walk away from the ferry terminal should turn right to follow the main road through Brodick. If any food or drink is needed at the outset, then there are a variety of shops along the way where supplies may be obtained. The main road hugs the rocky shore at first, then continues between the golf

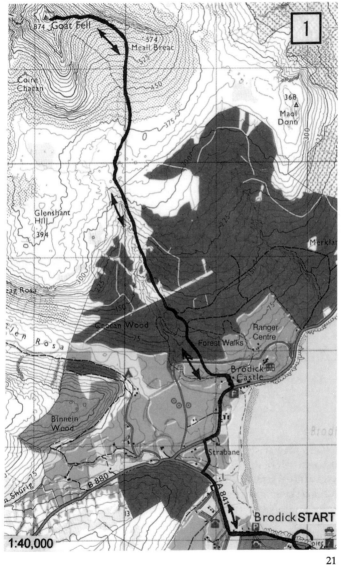

Snow-capped Goat Fell seen from Strathwhillan above Brodick Pier

course and Ormidale Park on the outskirts of town. Further along, the road passes Brodick Primary School, where a tall standing stone will be noticed across the road. Also across the road is the Arran Heritage Museum. Immediately before the museum buildings there is a public footpath signpost listing destinations such as Brodick Country Park, Brodick Castle and Goat Fell.

Follow the route indicated, which is a gravelly path between a beech hedge and brambles. Cross a footbridge over Glenrosa Water, then head straight onwards, following another path between a beech hedge and a golf course. This path leads back onto the main road, having cut out a slightly longer bend. Turn right to follow the road, which later bends to the left and passes a development of specialist shops dealing in crafts and foodstuffs. The road then bends to the right to reach the Cladach Sawmill and there is a public footpath sign on the left indicating the start of the climb to Goat Fell. Follow a clear track past the buildings of the Arran Craft Centre, continuing uphill through woods rich in rhododendrons and crossing a tarmac driveway which serves nearby Brodick Castle. Just across the driveway there is an information board detailing the extent of the upland holdings of the National Trust for Scotland on the Isle of Arran.

Follow the track uphill into Forestry Commission property. There is a small marker confirming that this is the way towards Goat Fell. As the track climbs, there are waymarked paths leading to left and right, but stay always on the clearest track and avoid these other trails. At a higher level, turn left at a junction of forest tracks, again indicated as the way to Goat Fell. When a crossroads of tracks is reached a little further along, go straight through. The path leads through an area where rhododendron scrub has been cut back, passing through an old gateway in a low drystone wall. The path climbs through an area where the stands of forestry are more distant, and rises on a bracken and heather slope where there are a few scattered stands of birch. The path remains quite clear as it climbs and there is a feeling that Goat Fell is becoming closer, but the path is rugged in places and eyes should be kept more to the ground. The path crosses a channel of water that has been cut across the hillside, then it reaches a gate in a tall deer fence. Beyond the gate the mountain is owned and managed by the National Trust for Scotland.

The path continues uphill at a gentler gradient for a while, and the surface has been restored in some places. There are areas of pitched stone and gravel, with drains removing excess water, although some parts cross bare granite bedrock. The surrounding moorland is mostly wet, grassy, heathery and bouldery. The gradient gradually increases as the path climbs up onto the shoulder of Meall Breac. There is a level stance before the path swings more to the left and aims directly for the summit of Goat Fell. This is the toughest part of the ascent, as the braided path crosses loose stones and gritty slabs of granite. There is a rugged ridge of rock on the steep ridge and walkers can choose whether to head uphill to the right or left. Care should be taken not to dislodge boulders as there are likely to be other walkers around, even if they are out of sight. The summit is reached quite suddenly and is composed of a bare table of granite bearing a few large boulders. There is a trig point and a view indicator has been provided by the Rotary Club of Kilwinning. Goat Fell is the highest summit on the Isle of Arran at 874m.

If a careful check has been made of progress so far, then walkers should be able to gauge whether they are going to catch their intended bus or ferry. The descent needs to be taken carefully at first, but it should take less time than the ascent. It is simply a matter of retracing steps all the way to the ferry terminal, although there is always the option of catching a convenient bus on the main road near the Arran Craft Centre at Cladach.

Arran Heritage Museum
The Arran Heritage Museum is based in a huddle of whitewashed buildings on the main road just outside Brodick. Collections of artefacts have been assembled by a voluntary group to illustrate living conditions on the Isle of Arran in the recent past; up to the 1920s. There is a typical cottage, smithy, stable block and numerous agricultural implements. There are displays relating to the island's geology and archaeology, as well as shipping and archive material. Facilities include a tearoom and picnic area.

Arran Craft Centre
Brodick has shifted from the northern side of Brodick Bay to the southern side. Old Brodick is remembered at Cladach; the huddle of old buildings near Brodick Castle. The Old Inn, the Village Inn, a woollen mill and a few houses were all that constituted the village. When the grounds surrounding Brodick Castle were redeveloped in 1853, the woollen mill was moved to Millhouse and the tenants were rehoused at Douglas Place and Alma Terrace. A new school was built in 1854. Tourists had already begun to visit the Isle of Arran, frequenting the Old Inn at Cladach, where goat's milk was a speciality! Tourism continued to develop, so that the new village of Brodick became equipped with a new and larger pier, a large hotel, shops and other businesses. Cladach has recently been redeveloped as the Arran Craft Centre, featuring a range of arts and crafts, but retaining the appearance of a small village.

WALK 2
Brodick Castle & Country Park

The towers and turrets of Brodick Castle are easily distinguished poking above forests on the lower slopes of Goat Fell. Castles have been built and rebuilt on this site for centuries, but the present castle dates only from the 19th century and was the seat of the Dukes of Hamilton. Brodick Castle is the centrepiece of the National Trust for Scotland's holdings on the Isle of Arran. It houses silverware and porcelain, paintings and sketches, with rooms full of fine furniture. Wrapped around Brodick Castle is a colourful woodland garden threaded by a variety of paths, lavishly planted with exotic trees and rhododendrons. A separate walled garden has a more regimented layout and features more flowers than trees. The grounds around Brodick Castle were designated as a Country Park in 1980

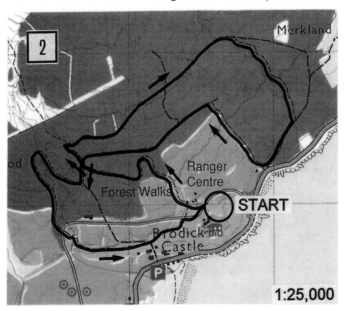

and are managed by the National Trust for Scotland and the District Council. There are rangers and a Countryside Centre, as well as a series of four colour-coded nature trails to explore. The following walk combines the waymarked trails to present a single long walk on the forested hillsides above the castle. There are specific maps of the trails which can be obtained from the Reception Centre or Countryside Centre, or simply studied on noticeboards at the start.

The Route

Distance:	5¹/₂ miles (9km)
Start:	Reception Centre, Brodick Castle, grid ref 017379.
Terrain:	Clear woodland paths and forest tracks, featuring colour-coded waymarks.

Use the main entrance to Brodick Castle and park in the car park beside the Reception Centre. There is information readily available when the centre is open, as well as toilets. Tickets can be obtained for Brodick Castle, which also houses a restaurant. The Castle is generally open from 11.30 to 17.00, April to October, while the Country Park is open all year from 09.30 until sunset. Tickets are also available for informative guided walks around the gardens.

Leave the Reception Centre, walk up a flight of steps towards the castle, but turn right along a path and follow signs for the Countryside Centre. The centre is in a huddle of buildings just above the castle and notices explain about the range of nature trails which can be followed. They are: the Merkland Gorge Trail with red markers; the Castle Parks Trail with blue markers; the Cnocan Trail with green markers; and the Lower Cnocan Trail with yellow markers. All four colours are displayed together at the start, while just off to the left is a tiny Wildlife Garden. A glance is all that is needed to observe the Wildlife Garden, with its pond, fruit and vegetable plot, wildflower meadow, woodland garden, herbaceous border and habitat piles.

Follow the colour-coded waymarked path uphill and away from the Countryside Centre, crossing a footbridge over a burn. Just to the left is a short optional loop called Wilma's Walk. A plaque explains:

Wilma Forgie was Joint Representative at Brodick with her husband John from 1973 until her untimely death in 1983. She was greatly loved by staff and visitors alike and left her mark on Brodick in many ways; one of them was the inspiration for this short walk. It has now been named after her so that those who follow it will remember her.

Wilma's Walk simply heads down through the woods, crosses the burn and ascends gently back to the Countryside Centre.

The colour-coded waymarked walks follow the path up through a gate, across a stile, and uphill again. Rhododendron scrub has been cleared and the woodland floor is light enough to support a riot of grasses and flowers, all vying with each other for attention. Cross a footbridge, then climb higher to cross another footbridge. The Mill Pond can be observed to the right, but the waymarked walks all head to the left and begin to run downhill, featuring views across Brodick Bay. The walled Hamilton Cemetery is seen to the left and it can be entered by a fine gateway. Slabs mark the graves of the Eleventh Duke of Hamilton, Brandon and Chatelherault, as well as the Twelfth Duke and his wife. Continue along the path until a junction is reached with a clear forest track.

Turn right as indicated by blue and red waymark arrows, then almost immediately turn left along a track marked only by a red waymark arrow. This track is also signposted for Goat Fell, rising gently before featuring a slight dip. Another red marker points to the right, leading walkers away from the line of the Goat Fell path. The forest track rises gently, but has no really decent views. A bench beside a small burn offers a chance to rest, and there is a fine view over Brodick Bay. The track rises a little more, then swings left, but a red marker points straight on along a grassy track. This track runs gently downhill, becoming gravelly before reaching a ford and footbridge. There is a turning space for vehicles just beyond.

Another red arrow near the turning space points out a path on the right which descends into Merkland Gorge. A loopy path has been carved into the hillside above the gorge, overlooking a rocky burn full of little waterfalls. Plenty of rhododendron scrub has been cleared in Merkland Wood to help revive what is one of the few ancient woodland sites remaining on the Isle of Arran. With light again able to reach the floor, seedling birch, pine and oak will be able to establish themselves. Sycamore and Douglas Fir will be controlled in accordance with a management plan established by the National Trust for Scotland and the Arran Natural History Society. Lower down the gorge, turn right to cross a bridge and follow a forest track almost down to the main coastal road. Off to the left, close to the road, is the relatively new Heronry Pool. A sign has been mounted near the pool, overlooking Wine Port. The rugged bay obtained its name after a French ship ran aground and its cargo of wine and silk was salvaged and taken up to Brodick Castle. The sign points out that the bay has a variety of wildife habitats, and includes notes about the red throated diver, black throated diver, great northern diver, pied wagtail, grey heron, oystercatcher, common sandpiper, red breasted merganser, eider duck, shelduck, mallard, grey seal and common seal.

A sign near the Heronry Pool reads "Merkland Wood Forestry Commission" and there is a vague path climbing uphill behind it. Trace this path carefully and keep climbing, avoiding any other paths which descend to the left. The path eventually drifts towards a fence and runs uphill between Merkland Wood and the pastures of Castle Parks Field. The path is actually the course of the blue waymarked Castle Parks Trail, but as it is being followed "backwards" it is important not to follow the trail in the "forwards" direction indicated by the blue arrows. The path turns around the top corner of the Castle Parks Field, then continues up through the woods on short flights of steps. The path becomes much clearer, bends to the left, then proceeds as an almost level grassy track. A gravel track is joined and this is followed gently downhill to cross a timber bridge. Keep straight on along the track until a junction is reached which may be recognised as one which was passed earlier in the walk.

Turn left and follow a clear forest track straight downhill. When the track bends to the left, take a right turn marked by a green arrow indicating the course of the Cnocan Trail. A broad path climbs uphill and runs across a slope overlooking Cnocan Burn. Cross a footbridge and enjoy a view of the Cnocan Waterfall. Continue following the path, observing more waterfalls on the way downhill. The green waymark arrows lead straight across a driveway serving

Brodick Castle, and the path running downstream offers a view of a fine stone arch supporting the driveway. Cross a footbridge which is flanked by flights of steps, then continue along the path which pulls away from the river. The path becomes a well wooded track and rises to a gate. Go through the gate and turn right along another track. Turn almost immediately left up a short flight of stone steps indicated by another green marker arrow.

A gravel path runs level and passes through another gate. A green marker then points left and uphill, with the path crossing a wide bridge over a narrow stream. Either follow a wide path uphill, or turn left to follow a narrower path closer to the burn. The narrower path crosses and recrosses the burn and is overlooked by some very tall and stately trees. Brodick Castle can be seen to the right, but the final green markers lead across a driveway and pass close to an adventure playground on the way back to the Countryside Centre. Walkers who have plenty of time to spare could explore Brodick Castle if it is open, or lose themselves on a veritable maze of garden and woodland paths between the castle and the main coastal road. One path running close to the road is known as the Lower Rhododendron Walk.

Brodick Castle
The foundations of Brodick Castle may be lost in time. It was garrisoned against Alexander before the Isle of Arran was ceded to Scotland, and there are some rather shaky stories and legends concerning Robert the Bruce and the castle. More solid dates of 1351 and 1406 cover the destruction of the castle by English forces, while Scots themselves attacked the place in 1455. After a rather chequered and battered history, the original features of the building are no longer available for study, and the castle has been in the possession of many families. The most notable owners were the Hamiltons; Dukes of Hamilton, Brandon and Chatelherault. The Victorian part of Brodick Castle dates from 1844. In 1853 the castle grounds were redeveloped and tenants in the old village of Cladach were rehoused where the more modern village of Brodick now stands. In an effort to pay death duties, Brodick Castle passed into the care of the National Trust for Scotland in 1957. Some 7000 acres of mountains around Goat Fell and Glen Rosa are also held by the Trust.

WALK 3
Brodick & Clauchland Hills

Lying between Brodick and Lamlash, the Clauchland Hills are a low range of hummocky hills under fairly extensive forest cover. A strip of ground of varying width has been left unplanted along the crest of the hills, while the whole of Clauchland Point has remained as tree-free pastures. A stroll over the Clauchland Hills could be accomplished easily from Brodick in a morning or an afternoon, but this particular route has been extended through Glenrickard Forest to return to Brodick by way of Glen Cloy. Further extensions could also be made in the direction of Lamlash, but there is another route offered in this guidebook taking in the Clauchland Hills from that side.

The Route

Distance:	9^1/$_2$ miles (15km)
Start:	Ferry Terminal, Brodick, grid ref 022358.
Terrain:	Good paths, tracks and roads through pastoral and forested countryside.

Start from the Caledonian MacBrayne ferry terminal at Brodick and follow the main road uphill signposted for Lamlash. The road climbs uphill, passing a garden centre, Strathwhillan Guest House and the turning for Strathwhillan. Continue uphill and the main road crosses a rise at the Carrick Lodge, then there is a minor road to the left at Allandale House which is signposted as the public footpath to Lamlash. This minor road rises and passes a sign buried in a hedge which announces Corrygills, but the scattered settlement only becomes apparent after reaching a crest on the road. The road runs downhill and passes a number of houses before the tarmac expires at a bridge. A clear track runs uphill to reach Dunfion, where bagpipe manufacture can be inspected at a workshop. The track continues around the hillside, with forest above and pleasant pastoral countryside below. When the track descends towards the

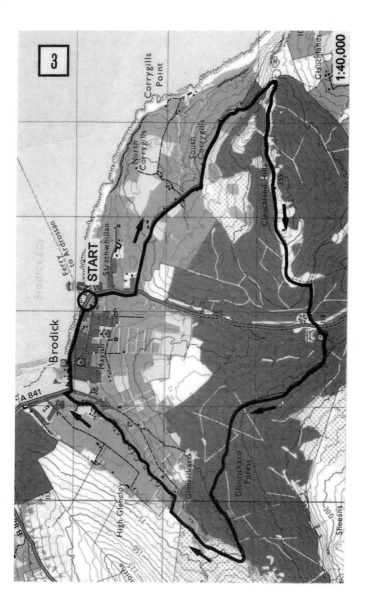

last building, there is a path off to the right just before the building. A sign announces this to be the public footpath for Lamlash.

Follow a short woodland path uphill, crossing a little burn beside a small water tank. A gate and stile give access to a forest, where a clear, stony path runs diagonally uphill across a slope. When the path leaves the forest it continues up and across the slope, with views only of the sea below and of the rounded hill of Dun Fionn ahead. The path reaches a little gap at the eastern end of the Clauchland Hills, where a fence divides the forest from a grassy, brackeny common. Turn right at a gate and stile to follow a path into the forest. A sign reads "Main Road via Clauchland Hills" while the other side of the sign gives directions for Brodick and Lamlash.

The path climbing uphill through the forest runs along a grassy ribbon flanked by bracken. There is a fairly steep pull uphill for a short while, and the trees are generally fairly close to the path. At a higher level the path is more of a switchback, rising more than it falls as it proceeds along the forested crest. There is a more significant gap to be crossed before the final pull up to the summit, and although the trees close in on the gap, generally they are well away from the path and there are later broad strips of heather to either side. There is a sizable cairn on the summit of the Clauchland Hills at 259m. A fine view extends across Brodick Bay to the highest mountains on the Isle of Arran. Unfortunately, because of the height of the trees, there is no corresponding view over Lamlash Bay.

The path leaves the cairn and runs along the broad ridge further westwards. Heathery, hummocky hills are crossed and the trend is gradually downhill. The path becomes a little steeper and stonier later, then runs close to the edge of the forest where it may be muddy in places. There are areas of bracken amid the heather, then there is a swing to the left and a view across Lamlash Bay after passing a number of young birch trees. The path reaches a junction where a sign reads "Cairn & Standing Stone". Look on the path to the cairn as an optional extra, leading along a forest ride with some squelchy spots to reach Dunan Mor Cairn, where a low mound and partial burial chamber can be inspected. If this detour is not required, then turn right at the sign and follow a clear, gravel path straight down

View indicator on the top of Goat Fell with rugged Cir Mhor beyond

A view from An Tunna across Lamlash Bay and Holy Isle (Walk 6)
A square tower lighthouse at the southern end of Holy Isle (Walk 7)

a rugged forest ride. The path leads to the main road linking Brodick and Lamlash at Cnoc na Dail.

There are a couple of picnic tables, a small car park, and signs indicating walking routes just off the road at Cnoc na Dail. There are also the remains of a stone circle to study. On reaching the road, the walk could be cut short by simply turning right and following it northwards down to Brodick. To continue the walk, however, cross the road and note a Forestry Commission sign offering routes to Glencloy Water and Brodick. The track behind the sign rises to a small car park and turning place, with a barrier across a forest track. Go past the barrier and follow a broad and clear, but rather coarse and stony forest track. The track rises a little and turns right, contours a little, then descends gradually through Glenrickard Forest. There are no real views, but in any case it is better to watch each footfall on the stony track. A smoother forest track later descends a little more steeply before levelling out later. It runs across a concrete slab bridge, before becoming a narrower path. There is a view around the rugged head of Gleann Dubh, taking in Sheeans and Creag nam Fitheach to the left and Sgiath Bhan to the right. A walk around the head of this glen is offered in Walk 4.

A signpost at the junction of the forest track and path points back along the track to Cnoc na Dail, as well as forwards along the path to Brodick. The path climbs only for a moment, then it winds along a forest ride as a clear ribbon of gravel. The ride is quite rugged, planted with grass, heather, bracken and bog myrtle. Follow the path along and downhill, then cross a footbridge over a burn draining Glen Ormidale. A faded sign at the edge of the forest reads "Absolutely no access beyond this point for bicycles or any other vehicles". Another sign for walkers coming the other way states that the path leads to Cnoc na Dail. The path running away from the forest is rough and cobbly in places, as well as a bit muddy. There is a field to the right and a rugged slope to the left, with plenty of bog myrtle growing on a wet area. The path is led between parallel fences towards a farm where horses are kept. A riverside track runs away from the farm, and there is later a sharp left and right turn along tracks offering a way out of Glen Cloy.

Keep straight on alongside the river to use a footpath through the glen. The riverside path can be muddy and stony in places, but it is always clear and walkable. A small development of houses are reached and their access road runs past the entrance to Auchrannie Country House Hotel and Country Club, which is open to non-residents. Continue along the road to pass an Army Cadet base, a garage, launderette, tearoom and Good Food Shop. A right turn on the main coastal road leads back through Brodick to the ferry terminal.

Brodick
Brodick's main features and facilities can be spotted on the way back towards the ferry terminal. In order of appearance they include: Connemara B&B, with the road to the right leading to Brodick Church of Scotland, Hotel Ormidale and Kilmichael Country House Hotel. Staying on the main road, look out for Brodick Golf Club facing Ormidale Park. Then come the Arran Library and Brodick Hall, Heathfield Hotel, Post Office, fire station, pharmacy, garage; supermarket, mountain bike hire, bowling green, craft shop, antique shop, Bank of Scotland, fast food take away and bakery. Everything else in Brodick looks across the main road to the sea, with ample parking slots all along the road. Everything else includes: Stalkers Restaurant, Invercloy Hotel, DIY store, toy shop, Arran Estate Agents, clothes shop, butcher, Tigh na Mara Guest House, clothes shop, craft shop, bookshop, leather goods, veterinary surgery, Royal Bank of Scotland, Brodick Health Centre, Dunvegan Guest House, Craiglea Court Holiday Apartments, gift shop, cafe, crazy golf, cycle hire, Kingsley Hotel and Duncan's Bar, Arran Hotel, Co-op supermarket, Douglas Centre (optician, dentist, outdoor shop and confectioner), Douglas Hotel and Ravis Bar. The hotel grounds include the *Arran Banner* newspaper office and Roman Catholic Church. Finally, all in a group, are the Caledonian MacBrayne ferry terminal, electrical shop, filling station, gift shops, fast food take away, bus terminal and Tourist Information Centre.

WALK 4
Sheeans & Glen Cloy

The Sheeans are the Fairy Hills, rising as rounded knolls above Glenrickard Forest. There is a very fiddly forest path and an awkward series of forest rides leading towards them, which need care in terms of route finding. There are no real paths over the exposed moorlands either, just a series of ill-defined sheep paths which could be linked together in some fashion. The route over Sheeans can be extended around the heads of Gleann Dubh and Glen Ormidale, before a steep descent is made into Glen Cloy, but the whole walk is best attempted in clear weather as the landscape could be confusing in mist. A prominent forest path and track are used to bring the circuit to a close.

The Route

Distance:	9 miles (14km)
Start:	Cnoc na Dail, above Lamlash, grid ref 018333.
Terrain:	Forest paths and tracks, but pathless moorlands where good navigation is required.

Start at the Cnoc na Dail forest car park, at the top of the main road between Brodick and Lamlash. Walk past a barrier gate and follow the stony forest track round to the right. Avoid the track to the left, but almost immediately after turning right, look left for a rather vague path through the trees. A boulder stands beside the forest track at the point where the path leaves it. Vague though the path is at first, it becomes clearer later, though fallen trees sometimes need to be crossed and there are other trees which are gradually encroaching on the path. The surface is either grass, moss, wood sorrel or pine needles. When a small burn is reached, the path swings left and runs more directly uphill. More fallen trees have to be crossed and there are more narrow stretches.

A turn to the right later leads into a wide clearing between the trees, but turn left to exit from the clearing and continue along another forest ride. The ride separates mature trees, to the left, from younger trees, to the right. The half-hidden remains of a fence can

35

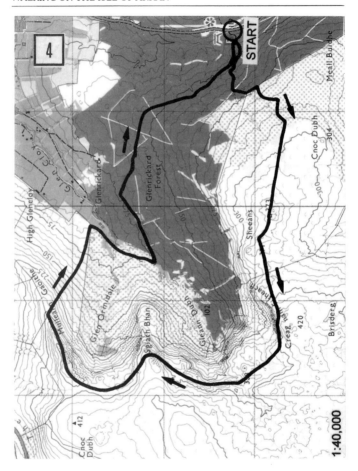

be spotted from time to time to the left. Turn right along a heathery forest ride and follow it uphill and across a broad crest. Soon after commencing the descent, turn right down another ride, passing plantations of younger trees, then rise gradually until a broad clearing is reached on the slopes of Cnoc Dubh. Follow another heathery ride to the right, then one to the left, to reach an exit onto

Muileann Gaoithe's summit seen rising above Brodick

a hummocky, heathery moorland. There is no fence at the top edge of the forest, so simply continue gradually uphill on the rugged moorland towards the humps of Sheeans. A short, steep, heathery climb leads to the summit trig point at 373m. There are views over Brodick and Lamlash Bay, as well as to the mountainous hump of Holy Isle.

Continue walking from the top of Sheeans, across a small, heathery gap, onto a neighbouring summit with a cairn at 371m. A broader gap is crossed next, and there is also a fence to cross on the next ascent. The aim is to climb uphill on a rugged moorland slope, keeping well back from the awkward cliffs of Creag nam Fitheach. Westwards lie seemingly endless rugged moorlands, where the walking can be quite difficult, especially in mist. The best strategy is to try contouring the moorland, heading roughly northwards at approximately 370-380m around the head of Gleann Dubh. There are a few small streams to be crossed, as well as a strange area blanketed in scrubby growths of willow. There is the chance to pick up occasional sheep paths, which can be linked to provide a route towards the prow of Sgiath Bhan. There is a small cairn in an area of boulders, and a vague path swings round the moorland slope behind the hump of Sgiath Bhan.

Contour around the moorland slopes at the head of Glen Ormidale, continuing across a broad gap between Cnoc Dubh and Muileann Gaoithe. There are two little summits on Muileann Gaoithe, the first with a small cairn and the second without. There is a clear path along the sharply defined ridge of Muileann Gaoithe, which can be followed down to a fence. Turn right away from the fence to descend into Glen Cloy. A steep slope of heather and bracken gives way to a gentler slope of tussocky grass. Walk down to a forest fence and continue downhill alongside it. Rampant growths of bog myrtle are passed. Cross another fence and a small burn to reach a path at the bottom of the slope.

Turn right to follow the path alongside the forest, reaching a sign where the path actually enters the forest. The sign indicates that the path leads back to Cnoc na Dail. There are views back around the head of the glen to Sheeans and Sgiath Bhan. The path reaches a broad track and a bridge in Gleann Dubh. Follow the track across the bridge, rising gently at first, then more steeply later. At a higher level, the track gradient eases, though the surface is quite coarse and stony. There are no real views along the way and eventually the track leads back to the car park beside the main road at Cnoc na Dail.

Cnoc na Dail

Cnoc na Dail means the Hill of the Meeting Place, reputed to be the place where crofters would meet regularly in the past to discuss matters of common concern. The word "Dail" has been preserved in modern parlance and is the name given to the Irish Parliament. The Forestry Commission has acquired all the land around Cnoc na Dail, providing facilities such as car parking, picnic tables, viewpoint and waymarked paths.

WALK 5
Lamlash & Clauchland Hills

The Clauchland Hills are a low range of hills between Lamlash and Brodick. Although they are largely under forest cover, a broad strip has been left unforested along the crest of the range, and the land extending to Clauchland Point is still a pleasant pastoral landscape. A circular walk based on Lamlash takes in the Clauchland Hills, Clauchland Point and the stretch of coastline leading back to Lamlash. Holy Isle is seen at close quarters and appears almost as a mountain marooned at sea. There is the option on this walk to make a detour and visit ancient stone remains. There are also options to use other forest paths and tracks to extend the route. This walk could be tied to another walk over the Clauchland Hills, offering an extension to Brodick (Walk 3).

The Route

Distance:	6 miles (10km)
Start:	Marine House Hotel, Lamlash, grid ref 033316.
Terrain:	Easy roads, tracks and paths through forest, over hills and along the coast.

Start from Lamlash, where parking is available at a number of places along the Shore Road. Leave town by following the Brodick road uphill from the Marine House Hotel. An old milestone might be noticed on the left just after passing the mobile homes on Park Avenue. Lamlash Golf Club and Caddies Tearoom are on the right just at the top edge of the town. Follow the main road alongside the golf course, reaching the highest tee (number five) before turning around to see Holy Isle completely filling Lamlash Bay. Most of the climbing along the main road has been completed, and there is simply a rolling stretch of road to be followed into Glenrickard Forest. A road sign indicates the arrival of a forest car park. This small car park is to the left at Cnoc na Dail, but the walk actually leaves the road by turning right to reach the Clauchland Hills.

A roadside Forestry Commission sign on the right indicates the

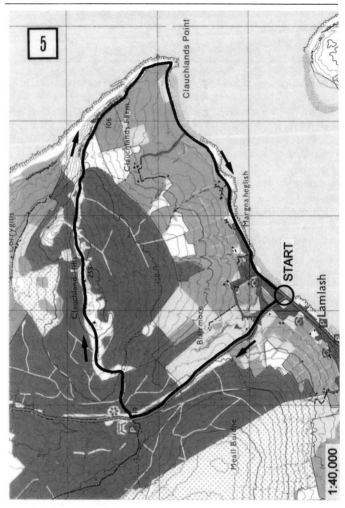

way forward for Corrygills, Brodick and Lamlash. The path passes a picnic bench on a heathery rise, and a short detour to the left would reveal the remains of a stone circle. The clear gravel path proceeds along a forest ride. The ride is quite roughly vegetated, but there is no problem following the path, which is firm and dry as it runs uphill. As the path emerges from the forest ride there is a sign pointing in two directions. The path to the left is marked as a forest walk, while a path to the right is marked "Cairn & Standing Stone". Look on the path to the cairn as an optional extra, leading along a forest ride with some squelchy spots to reach Dunan Mor Cairn, where a low mound and partial burial chamber can be inspected. If this detour is not required, then turn left and walk uphill along a wide unforested strip onto the Clauchland Hills. The path climbs uphill and there is at first a view back towards Lamlash Bay, but the path swings to the right after passing a few young birches and the view is lost. The path runs close to the edge of the forest for a short while and can be muddy in places. The path is steep and stony for a while, then it rises more gradually across heathery, hummocky terrain. The summit of the Clauchland Hills bears a large cairn at 259m. There is a good view across Brodick Bay to the highest mountains on the island. Unfortunately, because of the height of the trees, there is no corresponding view over Lamlash Bay.

There is a significant gap in the Clauchland Hills just beyond the summit, where the heathery swathes either side of the path become narrower and trees close in on the path. As the path proceeds along a switchback course, the trend is gradually downhill and the flanking ground is more brackeny and grassy. There is a steeper run downhill to the edge of the forest, where a sign stands beside a gate and stile. The sign points left to Brodick and right to Lamlash, but the direction to take is straight on, following a grassy path onto a domed summit crowned by a white trig point. This is Dun Fionn, the site of an Iron Age hill fort. Views across Lamlash Bay include the dramatic hump of Holy Isle. Note also the scrubby raised beach closer to hand near Corrygills Point.

The grassy path runs beyond the domed summit and proceeds down a slope of bracken close to a cliff edge. Various devices have been employed to protect farm stock from the cliffs. The remains of an earthen embankment, a drystone wall and at least two fences have all been constructed along the cliff line. Go through a gate into a field at the end of the point and proceed to an old concrete lookout post. There is a rocky protruberance offshore which is often used as a perch by gulls, cormorants and shags. A small quarry has been cut into the end of Clauchlands Point, and a clear track can be followed away from it. The track hugs the shore, passing another concrete lookout post and eventually joining a minor road at a corner. This road also hugs the shore and has a few small parking spaces along its length. Public footpath signposts at Margna heglish point back towards Clauchlands Point, as well as uphill towards Dunfion. The shore road is lined with houses and other notable buildings. The HF Holidays base is passed at Altachorvie, on a bend in the road. Swings and benches are passed near a bridge, followed by a derelict church. More swings and benches are passed before the road passes the Marine House Hotel and returns to the main part of Lamlash.

Lamlash

While Brodick may appear to be the capital of the Isle of Arran to casual visitors, the little town of Lamlash is actually the administrative centre, and also contains the High School, Hospital and Police Station for the island. The name Lamlash is derived from St. Las, who lived as a hermit on Holy Isle before becoming the Abbot of Leithglinn in Ireland. His name is also recorded as Molaise, and Holy Isle was previously called Eilean Molaise. As the island offers good shelter to Lamlash Bay, the place has been used on occasions to shelter entire fleets of ships. King Hakon of Norway assembled his fleet in the bay before his disastrous performance at the Battle of Largs in 1263. During the Great War, parts of the North Atlantic and Home Fleets also weighed anchor. Lamlash in its present form dates really only from around 1830. Families had been cleared from old clachans and new buildings were constructed to house them. The Parish Church dates from 1884 and was built by the Twelfth Duke of Hamilton. The Hospital was constructed partly as a war memorial and opened in 1922. The High School was completed in 1939, but did not take its first pupils until 1946. (See also Walk 6.)

WALK 6
Sheeans & The Ross

The Sheeans, also known as the Fairy Hills, are usually climbed using a forest path from Cnoc na Dail. There is another walk which climbs Sheeans on a rugged moorland route around the head of Gleann Dubh and Glen Ormidale (Walk 4). This route, however, takes in Sheeans on a rugged moorland route around the head of Benlister Glen. While this is a good option to consider when cloud blankets the higher mountains, it is not particularly recommended as an excursion in its own right in mist. The rough, exposed, barren, pathless moorlands require competent navigation. Much of the route is on moorland slopes, rather than on clearly defined ridges and summits. The route starts and finishes in Lamlash, but involves quite an amount of road walking at the start and finish. This can be cut dramatically by using bus services.

The Route

Distance:	8^{1}/$_{2}$ miles (14km)
Start:	Marine House Hotel, Lamlash, grid ref 033316.
Terrain:	Roads, forest tracks and paths, but also rugged, pathless moorlands.

Start from Lamlash, where parking is available at a number of places along the Shore Road. Leave town by following the Brodick road uphill from the Marine House Hotel. An old milestone might be noticed on the left just after passing the mobile homes on Park Avenue. Lamlash Golf Club and Caddies Tearoom are on the right just at the top edge of the town. Follow the main road alongside the golf course, reaching the highest tee (number five) before turning around to see Holy Isle completely filling Lamlash Bay. Most of the climbing along the main road has been completed, and there is simply a rolling stretch of road to be followed into Glenrickard Forest. A road sign indicates the arrival of a forest car park. This small car park is to the left at Cnoc na Dail.

Leave the Cnoc na Dail forest car park, and walk past a barrier

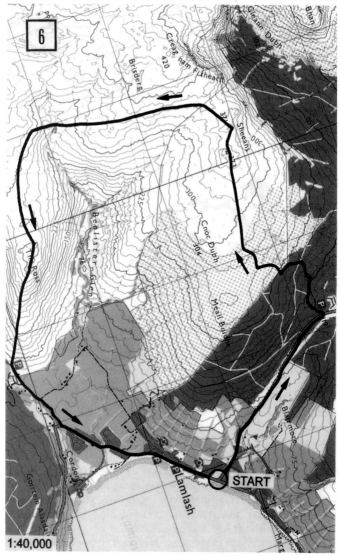

gate and follow the stony forest track round to the right. Avoid the track to the left, but almost immediately after turning right, look left along a rather vague path through the trees. A boulder stands beside the forest track at the point where the path leaves it. Vague though the path is at first, it becomes clearer later, though fallen trees sometimes need to be crossed and there are other trees which are gradually encroaching on the path. The surface is either grass, moss, wood sorrel or pine needles. When a small burn is reached, the path swings left and runs more directly uphill. More fallen trees have to be crossed and there are more narrow stretches.

A turn to the right later leads into a wide clearing between the trees, but turn left to exit from the clearing and continue along another forest ride. The ride separates mature trees, to the left, from younger trees, to the right. The half-hidden remains of a fence can be spotted from time to time to the left. Turn right along a heathery forest ride and follow it uphill and across a broad crest. Soon after commencing the descent, turn right down another ride, passing plantations of younger trees, then rise gradually left until a broad clearing is reached on the slopes of Cnoc Dubh. Follow another ride to the right, the heathery one, not the rushy one, then drift to the left, to reach an exit onto a boggy, hummocky, heathery moorland. There is no fence at the top edge of the forest, so simply continue gradually uphill on the rugged moorland towards the humps of Sheeans. A short, steep, heathery climb leads to the summit trig point at 373m. There are views over the peaks around Glen Rosa, Brodick and Lamlash Bay, as well as to the mountainous hump of Holy Isle and the broad moorland slope of Tighvein.

Continue walking from the top of Sheeans, across a small, heathery gap, onto a neighbouring summit with a cairn at 371m. A broader gap is crossed next, and there is also a fence to cross on the next ascent. Aim to climb gradually uphill on the rugged, pathless moorland slope, but also drift well to the left at the same time. There is no need to climb all the way to the crest of the moorland, but be content simply to pick a way across the slope in a roughly southerly direction. There are areas of tough heather, tussocky grass and boggy patches. It may be possible to see a pole on a broad moorland gap well to the right, but the route actually descends into a hollow in the moorland and crosses a small burn, just before it breaks into

Looking from Sheeans to the higher, mistier mountains of Arran

a series of waterfalls at the head of Benlister Glen. Once across the burn, climb straight up the heathery slope, still heading southwards, but then swing to the left to gain a broad grass and heather crest. Head eastwards, towards the summit of The Ross, which seems to stand directly in front of the shape of Holy Isle. The broad crest can be boggy in places, and there are some very vague paths. A short ascent on heather leads to a small summit cairn in a patch of short grass at around 310m.

Enjoy the views one last time. Holy Isle is well displayed in Lamlash Bay, with the broad shoulders of Tighvein filling the southern prospect. Westwards are empty moorlands and the dome of Beinn Bhreac, while northwards, beyond the Sheeans, are the jagged peaks of northern Arran stretching from Beinn Nuis to Goat Fell. The descent starts with a walk along the heathery crest of The Ross, passing another small cairn. Continue downhill more steeply, crossing heather and grass, then bracken on the lower slopes. There is a vaguely trodden path leading down to the road, but it is easily lost in the bracken towards the end. As there are also gorse bushes on the lower slopes, extra care is needed. Once the Ross Road has been reached, turn left to follow it across a cattle grid, passing the entrance to the forest walks at Dyemill, continuing past the Arran Provisions factory to reach the main road.

Turn left along the main road. If a bus comes along the road, then use it to return through Lamlash. If not, then walk along the road to return to whatever point was used as the starting point. Practically all the shops and businesses in Lamlash are passed on the walk from the Arran Provisions factory to the Marine House Hotel.

Lamlash

Features and facilities in Lamlash from south to north include: Arran Provisions, Westfield Guest House, Middleton Caravan & Camping Park, then a bridge. Over the bridge lie the Arran High School, coastguard, fire station, police and butchers. Then there is the medical centre and tennis courts, followed by a long, grassy sea front. After this interlude are Lamlash Parish Church, shops, Aldersyde Hotel, China Palace Restaurant, Lamlash Garage, shop, with the Post Office set behind a car park. The memorial to the Arran Clearances sits on a green backed by a terrace of white cottages. Then comes the Glenisle Hotel, Lilybank Hotel, Carraig Mhor Restaurant, pharmacy, craft shop, apartments, Pier Head Tavern, playpark and toilets, cafe, pier, marine stores, lifeboat, Arran Yacht Club, secondhand shop, video store, studio, bowling green, Drift Inn, shop/building society. After another long coastal green there is the Marine House Hotel. (See also Walk 5.)

Walk 7
Holy Isle from Lamlash

As the custodians of Holy Island we wish to preserve and enhance the natural beauty of its environment for the enjoyment of everyone. We ask for your cooperation in not smoking, taking alcohol or drugs, littering or making fires, and by respecting the island's unique flora and fauna.

This statement was taken from near the jetty at the northern end of Holy Isle, and it could well be applied to visitors throughout

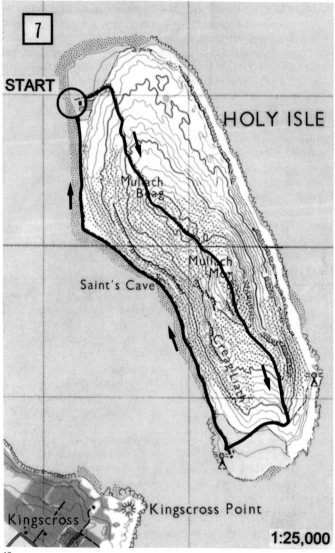

7

START

HOLY ISLE

Mullach
Buag

Mullach
Mor

Saint's Cave

Creag Liath

Kingscross Point

Kingscross

1:25,000

Arran too! Holy Isle has been bought by a community of Buddhists and has been designated as holy ground. As the community are willing to permit access to virtually the whole island, it is only fair that their wishes and beliefs should be respected. The route offered starts with a ferry from Lamlash to the northern jetty, rises along the crest of the island, visiting its summit at Mullach Mor, then descending to the lighthouses at the southern end. The return is along a clear coastal path, brightened with interesting and intricate rock paintings, and including a visit to a cave inhabited for twenty years by St. Las. It is also possible to visit the island using ferries from Whiting Bay, restructuring the route description accordingly.

The Route

Distance:	4^{1}/$_{2}$ miles (7km)
Start:	North Pier, Holy Isle, grid ref 053309.
Terrain:	A rugged hill walk on a clear path, followed by a clear, level, easy coastal walk.

The ferry from Lamlash to Holy Isle moors at a short jetty near a former farmhouse at the northern end of the island. On stepping ashore a plaque explains briefly about the Holy Island Project and one of the island residents may well meet the ferry and welcome visitors ashore. If walkers need any specific information about routes around Holy Isle, this would be a good time to ask.

There is a path rising through the field to the left of the farmhouse. It continues rising beyond a gate in a drystone wall, crossing bracken and heather where young trees have been planted. The path swings to the right and is marked by posts bearing arrows. Cross a stile over a fence and continue climbing uphill through more deep heather. The high mountains of northern Arran begin to rise above the low, forested rise of the Clauchland Hills. On a higher shoulder, Whiting Bay and the pyramidal island of Ailsa Craig appear in view. The path is narrow, but clearly trodden. It rises more steeply up a slope of heather, wrinkled boulders and outcrops of rock. The top of Mullach Beag bears a cairn and offers fine views around both Lamlash and Whiting Bay, while ahead the taller Mullach Mor beckons.

There is a short descent in two stages to a gap in the middle of Holy Isle. While a path may be noted sneaking off to the right, there is another path making a direct ascent of Mullach Mor. This stony path reaches rocky places where hands will be required for balance, though there are plenty of good holds. An easier stretch of path continues to the highest point on the island, where a trig point on Mullach Mor stands at 314m. The summit ridge is fairly narrow and composed of grass, heather, bilberry and rocky outcrops. Views take in most of Holy Isle, the forests and moorlands of southern Arran and the high mountains of northern Arran. A good stretch of the Clyde is also in view, along with Ailsa Craig.

The path runs roughly southwards, descending more and more steeply. There is one stretch where it picks its way down a slope of worn, broken rock. On a gentler shoulder, beware of a dark, deep, narrow fissure in the rock to the right. Stick strictly to the path as there are other hidden fissures. Note the cabin on the hillside to the right, which is inhabited by the Venerable Lama Yeshe Losal. The path descends one more rounded, heathery ridge, joining a clearer path in an area of bracken. A left turn at this point leads easily to a square tower lighthouse, though any continuation along the coast crosses rugged ground. A right turn leads towards a round tower lighthouse and the former lighthouse keeper's cottages. This route passes interesting rock paintings, on the right, before reaching a walled garden, on the left. The nearest room in the cottages is a Shrine Room and, after removing footwear, visitors are free to enter and look around. The lighthouse faces Kingscross Point, which is the closest point on the Isle of Arran to Holy Isle.

Retracing steps slightly, there is a grassy path leading through the bracken, running roughly northwards from the walled garden. Follow this path, which is also marked by the line of poles carrying electricity lines. While following the path, keep an eye open to the right, to spot a number of splendid rock paintings. These were executed by a Tibetan woman called Dekyi Wangmo, who was working to a series of traditional designs. One large painting of Buddha is accessible only by climbing a rope ladder! The path is slightly more rugged as it turns around a bay fringed with a few trees. Look out for steps to the right, rising to a cave at the base of a cliff. This is St. Molaise's Cave, and nearby is his Judgement Seat and Healing Spring. A ladle is provided for those who wish to taste the water.

The path is smooth and level as it turns around the shingly White Chorten Point. It is surfaced in short grass and runs through bracken which has been planted with young trees. The former farmstead at the northern end of the island is reached and the walk is brought to a close. It may be possible to join the residents for tea while waiting for the ferry. There is also abundant information about the Holy Island Project to take away. Donations to assist in the work being carried out on the island may also be made.

Holy Island Project

There are three parts to the Holy Island Project. The southern end of the island is being developed as a Retreat Centre. The northern end of the island is being developed as a Centre for Peace and Reconciliation. There is also a conservation element, involving bracken control and tree planting. Residents on the island include Tibetan Buddhist monks, nuns and lay people, as well as people of other faiths and volunteers helping with conservation or construction work. As the island has been designated as holy ground, residents take five vows - not to kill, steal, lie, indulge in sexual misconduct or take intoxicants.

St. Las

The most notable saint on Arran was St. Las, born in the year 566. He lived as a hermit in a cave on Holy Isle for twenty years before becoming the Abbot of Leithglinn in Ireland. His name is also recorded as Molaise, and Holy Isle was previously called Eilean Molaise. St. Las died in the year 639.

WALK 8
Tighvein & Monamore Glen

All walks on the flanks of Tighvein are rough and tough as there are no trodden paths across the hill. There is, however, a waymarked forest trail which runs from the Dyemill car park near Lamlash to the lonely moorland pool of Urie Loch. The loch is only a short walk from the summit of Tighvein and therefore the waymarked trail offers the easiest approach. Finding a way off the summit of Tighvein is reserved for those who can navigate competently across featureless moorlands, especially in mist. There is a route roughly northwards across Cnoc Dubh and Garbh Bheinn which allows a descent to the head of Monamore Glen without too much grappling with forestry plantations.

The Route

Distance:	6 miles (10km)
Start:	Dyemill car park, near Lamlash, grid ref 015297.
Terrain:	Forest tracks and paths are fairly clear, but there are also rugged, pathless moorlands to negotiate.

This walk starts at the Dyemill car park on the Ross Road outside Lamlash. The road is signposted for "Sliddery via Ross" off the main road south of Lamlash. The turning looks as though it is the entrance to the Arran Provisions food factory, as the factory buildings stand on both sides of the road. The road runs up past the Dyemill Lodges Holiday Homes, then reaches a forest track on the left. A sign beside the road reads "Forestry Commission. Dyemill. Car park & picnic area with forest walks to Lagaville, Urie Loch, Whiting Bay & Kilmory." There is a grassy area with picnic tables to the right of the forest track, with car parking available beside Monamore Burn.

Go through a barrier gate and cross a bridge over Monamore Burn. A sign on the left points along a track for Whiting Bay and Kilmory, and this track is marked as suitable for cyclists. A sign to the right indicates the "Lagaville Walks" and the hill walk to Urie

Loch. Follow the riverside path a short way upstream alongside Monamore Burn, then cross a footbridge on the right over a smaller burn. Turn left where another sign reads "Lagaville blue markers. Urie Loch red markers." Oak, birch and other trees alongside the burn screen a view of the more regimented forests alongside. There is one large beech tree beside the burn which spreads its branches wide to make the most of the available light. A footbridge on the left overlooks a small waterfall in a rocky gorge. Don't cross the footbridge, which is marked with a blue arrow for a rapid return to the Dyemill car park.

A red arrow beside the footbridge points uphill and care is needed in wet weather as exposed tree roots could be slippery. After passing the next red marker the path climbing uphill is stonier

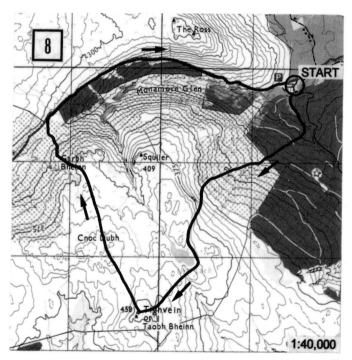

1:40,000

underfoot. The path pulls away from the burn and enters a mature stand of forest. It briefly returns to the burn and then enters a younger part of the forest where there is more light. The path running uphill is muddy in places and is flanked with heather and later with bracken as it climbs. There is a gentler stretch where the path is flanked by heather again, then a steeper climb is flanked with more bracken. This stretch of the path crosses a handful of small runnels, then it climbs up a forest ride which is mostly grassy. The path climbs up a steep slope of coarse grass, then cuts diagonally left across a heathery slope studded with a few boulders. The path actually runs along the top edge of the forest beneath the rugged slopes of Creag na h' Ennie.

A final red marker post at the top corner of the forest points across a rise of squelchy moorland. The path passes a couple of boulders and then runs down to the shores of Urie Loch. This is the end of the waymarked trail and anyone whose navigation is not up to scratch should consider retracing steps to the Dyemill car park. Those who can navigate confidently across bleak and pathless moorlands can continue over the broad summit of Tighvein and create a rough, tough moorland and forest circuit. Tighvein rises south-west of the head of Urie Loch, although there is no trodden path over the heather. The summit is not seen until at close quarters, but bears both a cairn and trig point at 458m. Views of the immediate vicinity embrace rugged, rolling moorlands. Northwards the higher mountains of the Isle of Arran are well displayed.

Leaving the summit of Tighvein, there is only a short, steep slope before more gentle gradients lead away towards the broad moorland rise of Cnoc Dubh. The heather cover is broken only by a couple of grassy areas, with even fewer small boulders poking through, and many channels of squelchy sphagnum moss. Side-step the channels where possible, but keep the ultimate objective of Garbh Bheinn in line. The prow of Garbh Bheinn is where the moorland slope gives way to forestry plantations at the head of Monamore Glen. Look carefully along the steep, heathery slope to spot a gap in the tree-line, where a forest ride can be accessed. Turn right along the ride, cutting across the slope, then turn left, walking down along another ride to cross a gap. A path of sorts heads diagonally uphill to the right along another ride, reaching the top of the Ross Road.

Turn right to follow the Ross Road downhill. There is forest on the downhill slope to the right practically all the way, but uphill is generally a steep slope reaching the summit of The Ross. At the bottom of the road, there is a turning on the right where a forest road leads straight back to the Dyemill car park where the walk started.

Lagaville

Lagaville was inhabited until the late 19th century, then the village was cleared and only some of the people were rehoused in Lamlash. Others emigrated to Canada. There is a monument on a green at Lamlash commemmorating the Arran Clearances. Behind the monument is a long row of terraced cottages built to accommodate people who once lived in places such as Lagaville. The Dyemill car park recalls the fact that there was once a water mill beside Monamore Burn, where cloth was finished.

Arran Provisions

There was once a water-powered meal mill at the foot of Monamore Glen. It was closed in 1967 and was demolished as the structure of the building was unsafe. The Arran Provisions factory occupies the same site as the old mill, and originally manufactured a range of quality mustard products. The factory now produces a range of fine jams and other preserves. Samples can be bought from the factory shop adjoining the visitor's car park.

WALK 9
Tighvein & Urie Loch

The highest point in southern Arran is the broad, bleak, heathery rise of Tighvein. All walks on its flanks are rough and tough as there are no trodden paths across the hill. There is, however, a waymarked forest trail which runs from the Dyemill car park near Lamlash to the lonely moorland pool of Urie Loch. The loch is only a short walk from the summit of Tighvein and therefore the waymarked trail offers the easiest approach. Walkers who enjoy crossing empty moorlands can extend this walk beyond the summit of Tighvein. Care is needed with route finding and relatively easy descents from the moorland are limited. Forestry almost completely encircles Tighvein and its neighbouring heights, and there are only a couple of ways down to the tracks which are hidden deep inside the forest. Forest tracks and other waymarked trails can be linked to provide a route back to the Dyemill car park, although there are options to head off in other directions, such as to Whiting Bay, Glenashdale or even distant Kilmory.

The Route

Distance:	7¹/₂ miles (12km)
Start:	Dyemill car park, near Lamlash, grid ref 015297.
Terrain:	Forest tracks and paths are fairly clear, but there are also rugged, pathless moorlands to negotiate.

This walk starts at the Dyemill car park on the Ross Road outside Lamlash. The road is signposted for "Sliddery via Ross" off the main road south of Lamlash. The turning looks as though it is the entrance to the Arran Provisions food factory, as the factory buildings stand on both sides of the road. The road runs up past the Dyemill Lodges Holiday Homes, then reaches a forest track on the left. A sign beside the road reads "Forestry Commission. Dyemill. Car park & picnic area with forest walks to Lagaville, Urie Loch, Whiting Bay & Kilmory." There is a grassy area with picnic tables to the right of the forest track, with car parking available beside Monamore Burn.

Go through a barrier gate and cross a bridge over Monamore Burn. A sign on the left points along a track for Whiting Bay and Kilmory, and this track is marked as suitable for cyclists. A sign to the right indicates the "Lagaville Walks" and the hill walk to Urie Loch. Follow the riverside path a short way upstream alongside Monamore Burn, then cross a footbridge on the right over a smaller burn. Turn left where another sign reads "Lagaville blue markers. Urie Loch red markers." Oak, birch and other trees alongside the burn screen a view of the more regimented forests alongside. There is one large beech tree beside the burn which spreads its branches wide to make the most of the available light. A footbridge on the left

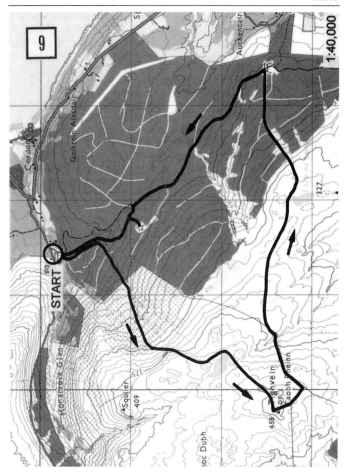

overlooks a small waterfall in a rocky gorge. Don't cross the footbridge, which is marked with a blue arrow for a rapid return to the Dyemill car park.

A red arrow beside the footbridge points uphill and care is needed in wet weather as exposed tree roots could be slippery. After passing the next red marker the path climbing uphill is stonier underfoot. The path pulls away from the burn and enters a mature stand of forest. It briefly returns to the burn and then enters a younger part of the forest where there is more light. The path running uphill is muddy in places and is flanked with heather and later with bracken as it climbs. There is a gentler stretch where the path is flanked by heather again, then a steeper climb is flanked with more bracken. This stretch of the path crosses a handful of small runnels, then it climbs up a forest ride which is mostly grassy. The path climbs up a steep slope of coarse grass, then cuts diagonally left across a heathery slope studded with a few boulders. The path actually runs along the top edge of the forest beneath the rugged slopes of Creag na h' Ennie.

A final red marker post at the top corner of the forest points across a rise of squelchy moorland. The path passes a couple of boulders and then runs down to the shores of Urie Loch. This is the end of the waymarked trail and anyone whose navigation is not up to scratch should consider retracing steps to the Dyemill car park. Those who can navigate confidently across bleak and pathless moorlands can continue over the broad summit of Tighvein and create a rough, tough moorland and forest circuit. Tighvein rises south-west of the head of Urie Loch, although there is no trodden path over the heather. The summit is not seen until at close quarters, but bears both a cairn and trig point at 458m. Views of the immediate vicinity embrace rugged, rolling moorlands. Northwards the higher mountains of the Isle of Arran are well displayed.

There are the remains of a fence south of Tighvein. Walk towards the fenceposts and turn left to follow them across the moorland. Beware of tangled pieces of wire in the heather. At a junction with another old fence, turn left and continue following the fenceposts. The posts lead down into a steep-sided little valley where a colony of foxgloves may be seen growing. Follow the fenceposts uphill onto a level moorland shoulder. Looking across the moorland to the right, two shades of vegetation can be distinguished and they are separated by a shallow ditch. Follow this line onwards, then later continue along a rugged, heathery crest to reach the lonely moorland pool of Loch na Leirg.

Walk around the left, or eastern side of Loch na Leirg, then walk directly eastwards away from the shore. The rugged moorland reaches a rounded brow overlooking the forested slopes falling towards Lamlash Bay and Whiting Bay. Look carefully along the rounded edge to locate a heathery notch which may be marked by a small post. Walk down from the notch towards the forest and look carefully for a vague path trodden between the trees, either across bracken or heather. The path is vague at first, but it does get much clearer and exploits a series of forest rides as it runs downhill. There is one place where a small burn needs to be crossed and there is a slight uphill stretch, but the path generally heads downhill and eventually emerges from the forest onto an area where gravel and stone have been quarried. There is a forest track just beyond with a picnic table on its crest. There is a fine view of the whole of Holy Isle filling Lamlash Bay. A nearby sign gives directions to Whiting Bay, Kilmory and Lamlash.

Turn left to follow the forest track downhill to commence the return to Lamlash, then after passing a junction the track climbs uphill. An area of birch trees stands on top of the track, and birch often screens the rest of the forest on the next downhill stretch. Look out for a sign on the left which indicates a path leading to Meallach's Grave. The gravelly path runs through trees and crosses a small footbridge over a little burn. It runs along a forest ride, then a white waymark arrow points left and uphill through more trees. A final grassy path leads to a pleasant clearing where four upright stones are located. This is Meallach's Grave.

Retrace steps downhill and turn left along the path at the next junction. The path reaches a concrete footbridge where a small sign indicates the remains of Lagaville Village, where only low, mossy, tumbled walls remain hidden in the forest. Turn right to follow the path downhill, passing a small pond and bench before following a burn downstream to a footbridge. Turn right to cross the footbridge, then turn left and follow a blue waymarked path downstream. There is a bench offering a fine view of a waterfall on the way downhill. At the next footbridge, do not cross, but turn right to reach a forest track. Turn left to cross a bridge over Monamore Burn to return to the Dyemill car park. Walkers without cars can easily walk along the road to reach nearby Lamlash.

WALK 10

Glenashdale Falls

There is a popular short circular walk which runs around Glenashdale Falls from Whiting Bay. It can be accessed either from Whiting Bay Youth Hostel, for a clockwise circuit, or from the Coffee Pot Restaurant, for an anti-clockwise circuit. The latter course is chosen for the following description, as the circuit is slightly easier in that direction. There is also the chance to extend the walk towards the end by climbing a flight of steps to reach a clearing where the ancient Giant's Graves are located. As with all waterfall walks, this walk lends itself to completion after a spell of heavy rain, when the falls will be at their most powerful. Another route visits Glenashdale Falls on the way to a longer moorland walk (Walk 11).

The Route

Distance:	4 miles (6km)
Start:	Coffee Pot Restaurant, Whiting Bay, grid ref 046255.
Terrain:	Easy roads, forest tracks and paths, with a flight of steep steps.

Starting from the Coffee Pot Restaurant in Whiting Bay, a public footpath signpost points straight up a road indicating the way to Glenashdale Falls. The road climbs, turns right and left, climbs further uphill and passes through a crossroads. Another public footpath signpost offers a number of destinations, including Knockenkelly and Auchencairn. The direction for Glenashdale, however, is straight onwards. The road rises slightly, then descends to pass some cottages beside a burn, before climbing again. The continuation of the road is along a farm track.

The track passes through three gates to reach a forest at a sign reading "Forestry Commission Forest Walks" giving destinations including Lamlash and Kilmory. There is a ford to be crossed, then the forest track rises gradually. Look out for a sign on the left which reads "Glenashdale Falls via Iron Age Fort", where a narrow path heads off downhill to the left. The path reaches a small viewpoint stance where there is a bench, overlooking the Glenashdale Falls in a lovely mixed woodland setting. Continue along the path, following white marker arrows, to pass the site of the Iron Age fort and eventually reaching the top of the waterfalls. There isn't a good viewpoint on this side of the waterfalls, so cross the bridge near a picnic table and turn left to continue.

The head of the falls are securely fenced to deter visitors from getting into difficulties. Cross a footbridge, then take a spur path off to the left, signposted as a viewpoint. Walk down a flight of steps to reach the best close-up view of the waterfall from a fenced stance. A short and long fall plunge gracefully into a deep, wooded gorge. Admire the waterfall, then retrace steps uphill and turn left along the main path to continue. The path descends through delightfully mixed, mossy woodlands, crossing a couple more little footbridges along the way. Eventually, a junction of paths is reached beside a ruined building and there is an option to climb uphill to visit the Giants' Graves.

There are 337 wooden steps climbing uphill on the forested

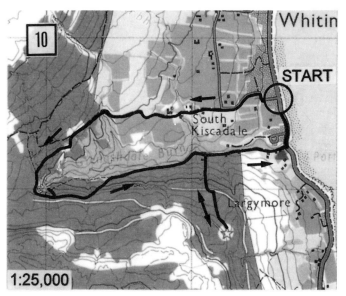

The Giants' Graves are a series of Neolithic burial chambers

slope. There is a gentler stretch beside a picnic table, then another steep path to a bench overlooking Whiting Bay. A dark and sometimes muddy path leads into a grassy clearing where the Giants' Graves can be inspected. These are Neolithic "horned gallery graves" and one of them has a clear passage and upright stones at its entrance. Retrace steps back down the wooden steps and turn right at the bottom. A clear, level path becomes a broad track, passing a couple of houses on the way out of the woods to reach the main road beside Whiting Bay Youth Hostel. Turn left along the main road to return to the Coffee Pot Restaurant.

Whiting Bay
Human habitation dates back thousands of years around Whiting Bay. The Giants' Graves are Neolithic and their construction suggests that there were communities in the area accustomed to working well together. At Kingscross there is a Viking burial mound. The area also has its share of stories concerning Robert the Bruce. He is said to have waited at Kingscross to see a signal lit on the Ayrshire coast, heralding a long and bitter campaign to gain the Scottish

crown. Two large farmsteads called Knockenkelly and Auchencairn paid rent directly to the king for centuries. The main road around the bay dates only from 1843, and there was once a pier built out into the bay (now demolished), and tourists were brought in by boats and wagonettes. To this day the village has a large number of hotels. (See also Walk 11.)

Giants' Graves
The Giants' Graves are found in a clearing high in the forest above Whiting Bay. They are of a construction known as "horned gallery graves". They are thought to have been used for the burial of people of close kinship in Neolithic times, with the bodies being placed into stone chambers which were then covered by large cairns. The "horns" are the upright stones flanking the entrances to the graves, creating a semi-circular forecourt which may have been a place where burial rituals were performed.

Glenashdale Falls
Glenashdale was well wooded before the Forestry Commission planted the higher slopes with conifers. The walk to Glenashdale Falls has always been a popular choice for a short, scenic stroll. The best time to view the waterfalls is after a spell of wet weather.

WALK 11
Glenashdale & Loch Na Leirg

There is a popular short walk above Whiting Bay which runs around the wooded, forested Glenashdale and includes a view of the fine Glenashdale Falls. This route is covered by another description in this guidebook. Walkers can increase the distance by climbing to the Giants' Graves above the bay, descending the same flight of steps as are used for the ascent. A more ambitious extension involves climbing out for the forest altogether, crossing bleak and empty moorlands around Loch na Leirg. There are trodden paths allowing walkers to reach and leave the moorland, but the high parts are quite pathless and need careful navigation, especially in mist.

The Route

Distance: 6 miles (10km)

Start: Whiting Bay Youth Hostel, grid ref 046253.

Terrain: Easy forest paths and tracks at a low level, but also an
exposed pathless moorland.

Start in Whiting Bay near the Youth Hostel at the southern end of the
village. There is a small parking space close to Glenashdale Bridge.
Signposts beside the road between the Youth Hostel and bridge
indicate the way to the Giants' Graves and Glenashdale Falls.
Follow the track past the last house and enter the forest. Another
sign confirms that this is the way to the Giants' Graves and
Glenashdale Falls. A little further along there is a parting of the
ways and a sign points left for the Giants' Graves and right for

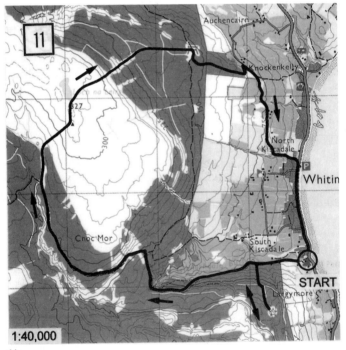

A view towards Beinn Nuis from the roadside near Kilpatrick (Walk 14)
Blackwaterfoot and Beinn Bharrain from the bouldery beach (Walk 14)

Walkers on Machrie Moor apparently heading for Ard Bheinn (Walk 19)
Bouldery stone circle on Machrie Moor with Ard Bheinn beyond (Walk 21)

Glenashdale Falls. A visit to both sites is recommended, starting with the Giants' Graves. A flight of 337 wooden steps climbs steeply uphill from a ruined building. There is a gentler stretch beside a picnic table, then another steep path to a bench overlooking Whiting Bay. A dark and sometimes muddy path leads into a grassy clearing where the Giants' Graves can be inspected. These are Neolithic "horned gallery graves" and one of them has a clear passage and upright stones at its entrance. Retrace steps back down the wooden steps to take another path to the left, signposted as leading to Glenashdale Falls.

There is a firm riverside path at first, then the path climbs uphill to cross a little footbridge on the side of Glenashdale. The path contours through pleasantly mixed, mossy woods. Cross over another little footbridge, where a slender waterfall can be seen in a rocky gorge. A signpost points to the right, indicating a viewpoint which is reached by descending a flight of steps to a securely fenced stance. Glenashdale Falls are revealed suddenly as a short and long fall over two sheer walls of rock. This is the closest view of the falls which can be reached in safety. Walk back up the steps and turn right to continue up the main path. This crosses another little footbridge and there is another fenced viewpoint overlooking only the upper part of the waterfall. A more substantial footbridge spans Glenashdale Burn above the waterfalls and there is a picnic table beside the river.

Follow the path away from the head of the waterfalls, taking note of a white waymark arrow where a short barrier fence has been built across a path. By following the white markers, a return can be made fairly quickly to Whiting Bay. To stick to the longer walk, however, disregard the white marker and walk along the path behind the short barrier fence. The path runs up to a clear forest track. Turn left to follow the track uphill, passing across a steep, heathery, rocky slope which has been left unplanted. The track climbs past an area where stone has been quarried, then it roughly contours around the forested hillside of Cnoc Mor. Look out for a picnic table to the right of the track, while a small waterfall can be investigated off to the left, on the rushing burn called the Allt Dhepin.

Turn right to leave the forest track and follow a path upstream from the waterfall. There is a clear path trodden through heather where a substantial strip has been left unplanted with trees. On reaching the edge of the forest the path expires on the rugged moorland beside the Allt Dhepin. Head roughly north-east from the edge of the forest, climbing up a rugged heathery slope. Look out for a small cairn on a heathery rise, then continue walking north-east, passing within sight of the lonely moorland pool of Loch na Leirg. Avoid walking too close to its outflow, where the ground is very soft and boggy.

The rugged moorland reaches a rounded brow overlooking the forested slopes falling towards Lamlash Bay and Whiting Bay. Look carefully along the rounded edge to locate a heathery notch which may be marked by a small post. Walk down from the notch towards the forest and look carefully for a vague path trodden between the trees, either through bracken or heather. The path is vague at first, but it does get much clearer and exploits a series of forest rides as it runs downhill. There is one place where a small burn needs to be crossed and there is a slight uphill stretch, but the path generally heads downhill and eventually emerges from the forest onto an area where gravel and stone have been quarried. There is a forest track just beyond, with a picnic table on its crest. There is a fine view of the whole of Holy Isle filling Lamlash Bay. A nearby sign gives directions to Whiting Bay, Kilmory and Lamlash.

Walk down the narrower forest track which is signposted for Whiting Bay via Hawthorne. The track is mostly stony, but it can be muddy in places. It runs downhill, passing through an old gateway in a wall and fence. After dropping through a dark stand of mature trees the track emerges into a lighter area and finally drops down to a narrow tarmac road at Hawthorne Farm. Turn right at a sign for Whiting Bay and pass the end of the tarmac road to continue along a stony track. Keep to the right to pass Knockenkelly House, as the track descending to the left is rather muddy. Keep straight on past Primrose Cottage, following the track along, then downhill, then right at a junction with another track. Houses are passed on the final run down into Whiting Bay. To complete the circuit, turn right along the main coastal road and walk back through the village.

Whiting Bay

Whiting Bay is a long and straggly village with two distinct halves separated by a gap. Working from north to south, features and facilities include: Burnside Caravan Park, Church of Scotland, football pitch and toilets, garage, Bay Stores, Trafalgar Restaurant, Argentine Guest House, Invermay Hotel, Burlington Hotel, Cameronia Hotel, Royal Hotel, Whiting Bay Primary School and a derelict chapel. After a gap there are the following features and facilities: antique shop, Norwood B&B, craft centre, car park, craft shop, newsagents, toilets, post office, pharmacy, grocers, Kiskadale Hotel, Pantry Restaurant, Whiting Bay Village Hall, mountain bike and boat hire, car park, Grange House Hotel, garden and furniture shop, Nags Inn, tennis court, Corriedoon Nursing Home, Eden Lodge Hotel, Belford Mill Warehouse, Whiting Bay Golf Club, Coffee Pot Restaurant, Stanford Guest House, shop, Glenashdale Bridge, Whiting Bay Youth Hostel and a caravan park. (See also Walk 10.)

WALK 12

Lagg to Kildonan Coastal Walk

The southern shores of the Isle of Arran offer a fine, rugged coastal walk with a strong feature at the Black Cave on Bennan Head. The usual approach to the Black Cave is along the coast from Kildonan, but there is another approach from Lagg. Combining these two approaches makes a good linear route and both ends of the walk have small parking spaces and bus services. Alternatively, arrangements could be made for a drop-off or collection at one end or the other. A circular route can be created only by following the main road back round between Kildonan and Lagg after completing the coastal walk. The road walk is something of an anti-climax and is not particularly recommended. There is, however, a point of interest along the road where the South Bank Farm Park offers a farm trail, rare breeds and tearoom.

The Route

Distance:	5 miles (8km)
Start:	Lagg Post Office, grid ref 956215.
Finish:	Kildonan Post Office, grid ref 017213.

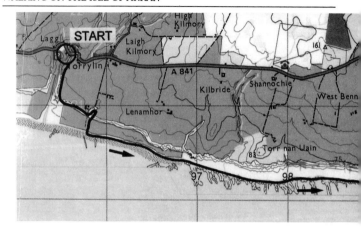

Terrain: Rugged coastal walking with some muddy patches. Some beach walks can be bouldery. The tide needs to be out at the Black Cave.

Start this coastal walk at Lagg, beside the Post Office and tearoom, across the bridge from the Lagg Hotel, where a signpost points the way to Torrylin Cairn. A clear gravel path rises through a woodland and runs along the edge of a valley. The path descends gently and swings to the left to reach a ladder stile. The stile gives access to Torrylin Cairn, the remains of which lie in a fenced enclosure. Cross back over the stile and continue along the path, passing a gate and stile before following a grassy track uphill towards a farm. The track bears left as it passes the farm, but another track on the right offers a direct line down to the beach.

Turn left to walk along the beach, passing the ruin of a hut which was built into a wall-like igneous dyke. Continue past a beach hut as well as a large container used as a shed in a field. The only access to a series of fields along the coast is from the beach, so there may well be tractor tracks along the shore. The beach becomes quite bouldery. Most of the boulders are curiously pitted and banded, and have obviously come from a couple of outcrops projecting above the sand, but there are also other large boulders which have

1:40,000

their origins from elsewhere on the island. Walk along the beach only until a waterfall is seen pouring through a rocky gorge before flowing to the sea. Come ashore at this point and go through a gate in a fence. A vague, grassy path can be followed onwards, and there are a couple more gates in fences to be passed through, and above each fence is a small waterfall. A beach of huge, rounded boulders is passed and the ground gets rather wet and muddy in places. Some areas have abundant growths of wild iris, but later there are areas of thorny scrub too.

A prominent igneous dyke is passed, as well as the ruins of a drystone wall. The ground gets rougher, wetter and muddier. There are boulders poking through the ground as the path picks its way beneath a blocky cliff and a blocky, bouldery scree. There are also a couple more igneous dykes running out to sea. A waterfall is passed, which plunges into a small stand of trees. Immediately after fording the burn below the waterfall, a substantial upstanding outcrop is passed and the bouldery point of Bennan Head is turned. The point can only be turned safely while the tide is out, as the boulders which need to be crossed are otherwise underwater and the cliff above the waterline is sheer and hoary with lichen. Just around the corner is the Black Cave, which is easily entered. It appears to have an exit at the back, but this is not recommended as an escape to the top of the cliff. The hole through which daylight enters is often damp, dripping with water and rather slippery underfoot.

Continue around the point on large boulders, then there is a choice of routes. Either walk carefully across the boulders uncovered by the tide, or walk at a higher level, linking bouldery and grassy areas to proceed. Neither way is particularly easier than the other, and care is needed to avoid a wrenched ankle or a fall. Some of the boulders on the shore can be slippery with fine seaweed, while some of those above the water line can be covered in an amazing variety of lichens. It is eventually better to come ashore and stay ashore. A path proves to be rugged at first, but it gets better after passing a ruined drystone wall. The way ahead can be grassy and muddy, with more patches of wild iris, as well as rushy or brambly areas. Looking to the sea, note the vast number of igneous dykes running across the bouldery beach. There are a couple of slender waterfalls off to the left, with a larger fall seen before a gate is reached. Continue walking along the path, which gets easier and easier, passing through three more gates. A track is reached at the Kildonan Stores and post office, and again there is a waterfall just behind the buildings. The rest of the scattered village of Kildonan can be walked through by following the road if desired. Views to sea include the little island of Pladda and its lighthouse, with Ailsa Craig beyond.

Torrylin Cairn
Much of the stonework from the Torrylin Cairn has been plundered as building material, leaving only a fraction of the original burial chamber and cairn behind. The cairn is said to be characteristic of the "Clyde" cairns found throughout this part of Scotland. The chamber was excavated in 1900, when it was discovered that only the innermost stone compartment was undisturbed. The remains of six adults, a child and an infant were identified, along with a small flint tool and a fragment of a pottery bowl. The Isle of Arran had been settled for at least 2700 years by the time the Torrylin Cairn was constructed. This and other similar monuments indicate the development of small, dispersed agricultural settlements with a high degree of community involvement.

Black Cave

Before the Isle of Arran raised itself from the sea after the Ice Age, as evidenced by its encircling raised beaches, the Black Cave must have been permanently full of sea water. Even now at high water the sea laps just inside the cave. A roof fall seems to have created the back exit from the cave, and a steep slope of bouldery debris has remained. When the sea was able to enter more of the cave in the past, this may well have been a blow-hole.

Kildonan

Kildonan derives its name from St. Donan, who arrived on the Isle of Arran with St. Columba in the 6th century. He is buried in the area and there are the remains of an ancient chapel still visible. The mouldering ruins of a castle can also be inspected, though little is known of its early history. It was a property of the Stewarts, but passed to the Hamiltons in the 17th century. The present village of Kildonan is a scattered affair, and of relatively recent origin, as previously the people in the area lived in primitive clachans. Walking along the shore road reveals most of the features and facilities, which from west to east include the following: Kildonan Stores and Post Office, a war memorial on an igneous dyke, car park, Breadalbane Hotel, Breadalbane Lodge Park Camping and Caravanning Site, Drimna Lodge Guest House and Kildonan Hotel.

WALK 13

Kilmory Forest Circuit

Much of southern Arran is under forest cover and the walking tends to be rather similar in many places. There is an interesting forested circuit north of the village of Kilmory, where an old track which has grown quite wild can be linked with a more regular series of forest tracks. There are also options to make diversions to look for an ancient stone circle and a burial cairn hidden deep in the forest. The walk can be conveniently started from the main road at Kilmory, near the Torrylin Creamery, but it is perhaps better to start from Lagg, which has food and drink and gives walkers the option of

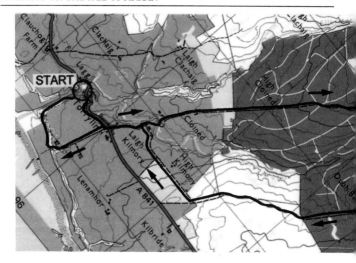

including the Torrylin Cairn in addition to the forest walk. The circuit described is essentially low level, but there are some parts which can be rough and muddy, especially in wet weather.

The Route

Distance:	12 miles (19km)
Start:	Lagg Post Office, grid ref 956215.
Terrain:	Forest tracks and paths, mostly firm and dry, but sometimes rough and muddy.

Start at Lagg, where the Lagg Hotel and Wishing Well Restaurant stand on one side of a bridge, while the Post Office and tearoom stand on the other side. Follow the road which zig-zags uphill from the Post Office and tearoom, passing the Kilmory Public Hall and Kilmory Primary School. Look out for the Island Porcelain building on the left, then later turn left where a narrow road is signposted for the Kilmory Workshop. The road runs along and downhill to reach Kilmory Church. There is a track signposted for the Kilmory Workshop just below the church. The track runs downhill a short way and crosses a bridge, then climbs uphill, flanked by hedges and

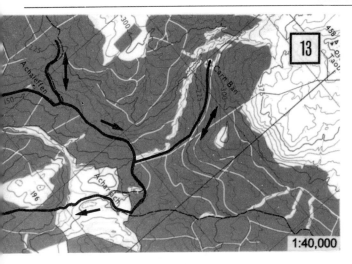

passing a series of fields. The Kilmory Workshop is at the top of the track at Cloined, where woodwork and pottery crafts may be inspected. Cars driven up the rough track to visit the workshop have a small parking space alongside.

The track proceeds beyond Cloined and the Kilmory Workshop, descending gently and continuing to be flanked by hedges, but it is now grassy and muddy in places. The track reaches a forest and there is a temptation to turn left, but in fact the direction to walk is straight onwards. Push past a handful of saplings to discover a hidden track. The track can be grassy, mossy, heathery, boggy, muddy, or even closed by fallen trees, but it is always clearly defined and shows signs that walkers are using it fairly regularly. After a bit of a struggle, there are two forest rides ahead. Keep to the right, still following a clear path along the ride. There are a few more fallen trees to be passed, and the grassy ride can be wet and muddy in places. Suddenly, a gravel turning space is reached and a clear, firm forest track continues onwards. The track passes the isolated farmstead of Achaleffen, which is no more than a house, outbuildings, small field and a little waterwheel. Walk straight past Achaleffen and keep following the forest track.

There is a forest track to the left which is signposted for the Achaleffen Standing Stones. The short detour to visit the stones involves following the track uphill. Four blocky stones stand in a little clearing to the left. They are signposted, but are not apparent until close at hand. Anyone not making the detour can continue along the lower forest track. There is another signpost to the left, just after crossing the little burn called the Allt an t'Sluice, indicating a path along a forest ride to Carn Ban. This detour is a little tougher than the previous one. First, a path along the ride has been made a little easier because a drainage ditch has been cut and a mound of earth and stones offers a good footing. Halfway to Carn Ban, there is a signposted left turn along another ride, where the grassy path can be wet and muddy in places. A sign to the left of the ride later offers a few details about Carn Ban, which is revealed as a bouldery burial mound whose upright entrance stones have been toppled. It is necessary to retrace steps back down the forest ride to return to the forest track afterwards.

Continue along the forest track, avoiding another track on the right. Cross a burn and continue to another track junction. A sign points left along a track, giving a cross-island option to Whiting Bay and Lamlash. Another sign points to the right indicating the way to Kilmory. Take the right turn, where the track leaves the forest and passes heathery ground around the isolated farmstead of Achariach. The track keeps left to avoid the farm, then drops down to cross a burn. It then runs uphill back into the forest and later falls gradually towards the exit. The track leaves fairly tall trees, then has younger trees to the right and heather moorland to the left. Looking back later, a Forestry Commission sign gives destinations all the way back to Whiting Bay and Lamlash. After a fairly level run the track drops downhill and is flanked by gorse bushes.

Turn right along another track, which is firm and dry for only a short distance. Its continuation straight on and downhill is wet and muddy; a sort of trough between hedges. There is another firm and dry track passing Kilmory Farm House, and when this suddenly turns to the left a rougher track continues straight on. The rougher track runs down to a minor road at Kilmory Church, and the minor road leads back to the main road. Turn right to return directly to Lagg. Alternatively, turn left almost immediately after making the right turn to follow a farm track towards the sea. The track passes one farm, then turns right around another farm overlooking the sea. Continue along the track, which is now more grassy and may be muddy. It eventually turns left and disperses into a field, but there is a gate on the right at the turning, and a path leads to the Torrylin Cairn. Cross a step stile to inspect the burial cairn, then continue along the path as it contours round above a wooded valley. There is a slight ascent on this clear path, then a descent to the post office and tearoom at Lagg. The Lagg Hotel is to the left, across the bridge.

Carn Ban
Hidden in a forest clearing reached only by following a forest ride, this bouldery Neolithic chambered tomb was used for communal burial about 5300 years ago. A Mesolithic hunting camp has also been discovered nearby, taking signs of human activity on the Isle of Arran back 8000 years. The main burial chamber was excavated in 1902 and was discovered to be divided into four compartments. Small fragments of bone and two stone tools were retrieved. A possible second burial chamber at the downhill end of the cairn has not been excavated. The existence of a burial cairn of these proportions, and their obvious frequent use indicates that the inhabitants of Arran at the time were living in fairly well structured communities with a great sense of purpose.

Torrylin Creamery
The Torrylin Creamery building beside the main road in Kilmory is sometimes open to visitors. Traditional Arran cheeses are made by hand and the process can be observed from a viewing gallery. Products can be bought on site at the adjoining Visitor's Shop. When the creamery opened in 1947 the entire Royal Family paid a visit.

Torrylin Cairn
See Walk 12.

WALK 14

Sliddery & Cnocan Donn

Between Sliddery and Blackwaterfoot is a hill called Cnocan Donn which is half rugged moorland and half forest. It provides exceptional views in fine weather for such a lowly height. Walkers who cross the hill could pick a way back around Brown Head on a patchy, rugged coastal path. There are features of interest at either end, such as the Preaching Cave near Blackwaterfoot and Torr A' Chaisteal Dun at Corriecravie. There are no real facilities along this stretch of road apart from a garage and a couple of bed and breakfast establishments, along with regular bus services.

The Route

Distance:	8 miles (13km)
Start:	Sliddery, grid ref 931229.
Terrain:	Roads, tracks, a rugged moorland walk and a bouldery coastal walk with some good paths.

Sliddery is a little village on a bend in the main coastal road. There is something of a crossroads on the bend, with a track running downhill and a minor road running uphill from a small red postbox Follow the minor road uphill, passing a handful of houses and farms. The road rises, falls and rises gently again to a cattle grid. Turn left to follow the road to a farmyard, then turn right along a clear track running across Corriecravie Moor. Walk to a rise on the track, where there is a gate to the left. This gives access to a rugged moorland walk alongside Kilpatrick Forest.

Walk uphill alongside the forest fence, or some distance away from it, to make use of a series of very vague paths. There is tussocky grass, a little bog, an abundance of heather and bracken on the slope, as well as a scattering of boulders. A short detour away from the forest fence can include the undistinguished top of Cnoc Reamhar. Walk back to the forest fence to go through a gate in an electric fence, then follow the forest fence across a squelchy gap and over a heathery rise. There is another descent to another rather wet gap,

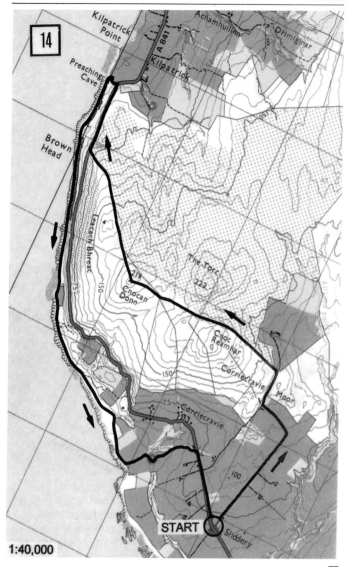

14

Kilpatrick Point

Achamhullin

Drimignar

A 841

Kilpatrick

Preaching Cave

Brown Head

Leacach Bhreac

The Tors
222

219

Cnocan Donn

Choc Reamhar

Corriecravie Moor

150

75

Corriecravie

100

START

Slidderry

1:40,000

where four fences join. Straight ahead are the heathery slopes of Cnocan Donn, which are crowned by a trig point at 219m. From this lowly eminence, there is actually an extensive view. The highest peaks of northern Arran stretch from the Pirnmill Hills to those around Glen Rosa, crowned by Goat Fell. The lower hills and moorlands of southern Arran stretch from Ard Bheinn to Tighvein. Ailsa Craig and the coast of Ayr and Galloway can be seen, along with Antrim, Kintyre and Jura.

Head back towards the forest fence and continue walking downhill. There is an easy, bulldozed strip beside the forest fence, leading down to a gateway on the main coastal road. Turn right along the road as if walking to Blackwaterfoot. When the road bends suddenly to the right, leave it by following a vague path to the left. This path runs between a wall and fence, and a bank of bracken. The going is decidedly tough later, and involves dropping down a rocky slope. Look out for a vague path on the left which leads down to a grassy strip beside a bouldery beach at the foot of a low cliff line. Turn left to follow the path.

There are a couple of caves in the low cliff line, including the smoke-blackened Preaching Cave. There is a good grassy path to follow for a while, but it gets more and more overgrown later with grass, heather, bracken, brambles and even honeysuckle and clumps of thrift. Transfer to the bouldery beach to continue, taking care while hopping from boulder to boulder. Looking uphill and along the cliff, little can be seen of the road, although traffic may be heard. Looking ahead, only one corner of the road can be seen, and on the shore around that point the walking becomes easier again.

It is possible to walk along a narrow, grassy path again, although it can feel cobbly underfoot in places, as the raised beach isn't far beneath the grass. There is a view of Ailsa Craig ahead, while out to sea seals may be hauled out basking on large boulders. Some wet and muddy parts of the path are flanked by wild iris. There is a drift inland from the shore on a broader, cobbly path, to the foot of a brackeny slope overlooked by a white house. When this path reaches a gate into a field, detour to the right around the corner of a fence to continue. The path runs out into an area of reeds followed by a grassy area studded with boulders. Cross the tangled end of a fence on the beach, then walk through more reeds, then turn left through a gate.

A line of wild iris in a field marks the course of a small burn which is followed upstream. Ahead is the prominent knoll of Torr A' Chaisteal, which has a grassy track slicing across its face. Follow the track uphill to have a look at an information board explaining about this ancient dun. The grassy track becomes vague at times, but it climbs along the edge of fields overlooking a valley full of hawthorns and other trees. When an old cottage is reached, cross over a stile to reach the main road. Turn right to follow the road over a rise, then descend to return to Sliddery.

Preaching Cave
The Preaching Cave is a fairly spacious, smoke-blackened cave cut into the low cliff-line below Kilpatrick. It is said to have been used for church services and there are also stories of it being used as a schoolroom at a time when the area was very poor.

Torr A' Chaisteal Dun
The natural grassy knoll at Torr A' Chaisteal bears the remains of a thick-walled dun which was built around 1800 years ago. The dun was a defended farmstead, situated next to an area of good agricultural land, yet close to the resources offered by the sea. The interior was partially excavated in the 19th century, producing human bones, a stone quern, pieces of haematite iron ore and midden material.

WALK 15
Tighvein & Glenscorrodale

To many walkers, Tighvein seems unapproachable. Maps suggest that it is flanked on all sides by pathless, featureless moorlands, and this is at least partly true. It also appears, from a study of the map, to be almost surrounded by forestry plantations, yet it is still possible to side-step them and enjoy the best of the wilderness moorlands. While paths may be few, the summit can be approached simply by climbing uphill until there is nothing left to climb.

Leaving the summit can be simplified by following the remains of a prominent fence across the moorlands. The whole circuit is based on the lonely farmstead of Glenscorrodale. The only public transport through the glen is an occasional Post Bus service.

The Route

Distance:	8 miles (13km)
Start:	Glenscorrodale, grid ref 963279.
Terrain:	Mostly rugged, pathless, heather moorlands and bog, with an awkward river crossing.

The farmstead of Glenscorrodale is the starting point, though parking is quite limited nearby. Follow the Ross Road towards the forested head of the glen, where the road twists and turns as it gains height. A derelict building will be noticed off to the right. There is a cattle grid at the top of the Ross Road, but don't cross it. Leave the road a little earlier by cutting sharply down to the right. There is a path of sorts cutting diagonally through a heathery ride in a young plantation of forest. Walk across the bottom of the gap and head straight uphill along another short forest ride, then turn right along yet another ride. Exit to the left and walk straight uphill as soon as a gap leading onto a heathery slope is spotted. Walk steeply uphill for a short while following a vague path on the rugged slopes of Garbh Beinn. The slope becomes less steep, but it remains rugged, pathless moorland towards the broad rise of Cnoc Dubh and onwards to Tighvein. The heather cover is broken only by a few grassy areas, with even fewer small boulders poking through, and many channels of squelchy sphagnum moss. Side-step the channels where possible, but keep the ultimate objective of Tighvein in line.

The summit of Tighvein has two distinct tops; one with a trig point at 458m and the other with a cairn. Views take in the immediate bleak moorland surroundings and extend to embrace the mountainous northern half of the Isle of Arran. Just beyond the summit is the line of a ruined fence, featuring decaying posts and straggly, broken wires. Walk towards the fence and turn right. The fenceposts form a continuous line across the moorland and are a great help with navigation away from Tighvein in poor visibility. A narrow ditch accompanies the fence as it runs down a rugged

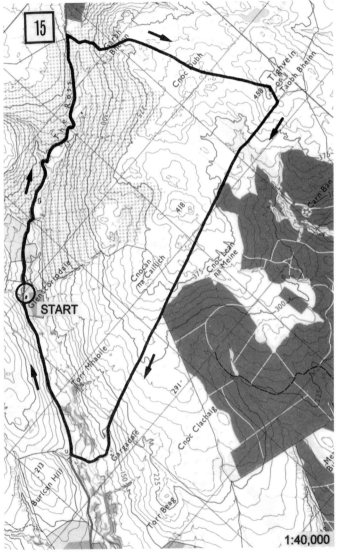

1:40,000

The broad moorland slopes of Tighvein rise above Glenscorrodale

moorland slope. Beware of any bits of wire which might be tangled in the grass and heather. A stream has to be crossed in a little valley, then the line of the fence runs along the edge of a forest for part of the next ascent. There is a stretch of ups and downs across a rugged hillside, before a more continuous descent commences. A junction is reached with another well maintained fence and it is necessary to pass through a gateway at that point. Continue following the fence straight downhill, running alongside another stand of forestry. A point is eventually reached where the fence turns left.

Leave the course of the fence at the corner, navigating straight onwards across a rugged, pathless moorland slope. There may be a few sheep paths which can be linked to provide a good footing across the heather, but these are not continuous and may ultimately lead off-course. The aim is to chart a course for the ruined village of Gargadale, leaving the gently sloping moorland slopes and dropping a little more steeply to get there. The heather gives way to more grassy slopes as a shallow valley full of tree scrub is entered. There is a landmark across the valley in the shape of a rectangular stone-walled sheepfold, while further down the valley, across a small burn, the ruined houses and walls of Gargadale eventually become visible.

The ruins of Gargadale can be explored, then it is best to cross back over the small burn to continue downhill. The remains of an old track fording Sliddery Water can be distinguished on either side of the river. Wet feet are to be expected at this point, while in wet weather a crossing may not actually be possible. Ford the river and climb uphill to join the Ross Road. (If this point can't be forded safely, then continue downstream, keeping above the river, to reach a road bridge at the next farm. Wise walkers would check its flow before starting this walk!) Turn right to follow the Ross Road. The isolated farmstead of Glenscorrodale is the only building along the road, so when it is noticed the end of the walk is in sight.

Gargadale

Gargadale's gaunt ruins are all that survive of a small clachan tucked away in a fold in the hillside. There is rather more shape and form to these ruins than to other deserted villages around the Isle of Arran, as more stone seems to have been used in its construction, rather than sods of peat. Unfortunately, unlike some of the other settlements, little is known about the fate of the tenants who were cleared from the land, although it has been suggested that they may have gone to Canada and settled at Cahleur Bay near Prince Edward Island.

WALK 16
The Ross & Cnoc a' Chapuill

Glenscorrodale is threaded by the Ross Road, whose only public transport is an occasional Post Bus service. Most of the upper parts of the dale have been forested in recent years, but much remains open, both along the length of the dale and on the higher ground. This walk takes a look at the extensive unforested moorlands to the north of Glenscorrodale, crossing the broad and pathless slopes of Cnoc a' Chapuill. The road is used through Glenscorrodale, while an old track is used to access the higher moorlands. A couple of fences form useful guides, but this walk is really for competent navigators, especially in misty weather.

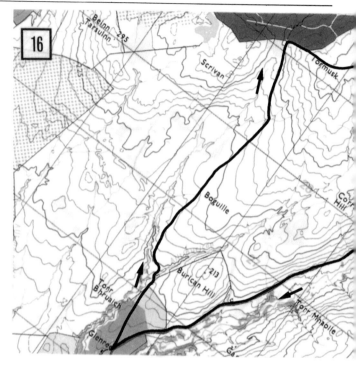

The Route

Distance: 10 miles (16km)
Start: Glenscorrodale, grid ref 963279.
Terrain: Roads and a vague track, but also extensive, pathless, rugged moorlands.

Park anywhere along the Ross Road between its highest point and the farm of Glenree. Parking somewhere near the remote farmstead of Glenscorrodale is a good idea, so that the road-walking is split between the beginning and end of the day. Walk away from the farm, following the road towards Glenree. The road is unfenced and crosses some rugged slopes overlooking Sliddery Water. Later, fences are noticed off to the right on the slopes of Burican Hill,

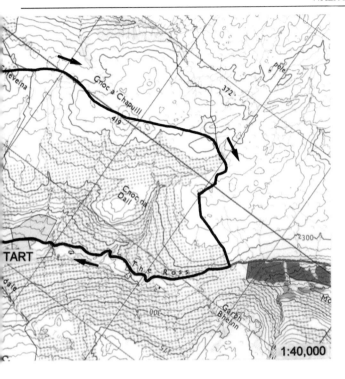

1:40,000

enclosing three large fields.

When the access track to Glenree is reached beside a stand of trees on the right, turn sharply right through a gate to follow a grassy track. The track passes through the three large fields, but the way ahead is vague. Look ahead to spot three gates, all slightly off to the left, and a fine track will materialise which crosses the Allt Burican near some trees. While the course of the track is very clear at this point, its continuation needs care. Follow the track uphill and it bends to the left. It becomes no more than a vague groove running through grass, heather and bracken. There is a swing to the right and it proceeds roughly northwards across the broad slopes of Boguille.

The track rises very gently across the moorland slope and cuts a fairly clear line across the slope at times. Quad bikes have been ridden alongside and a few walkers have trodden a narrow path. There is also a sparse line of short metal posts along the way. Only one small burn of any note is crossed, where a small willow is growing. Eventually, the track reaches a gap in the broad moorlands where a spiky line of forest trees can be seen even from a distance. There is a gate and stile at this point, but they should not be passed.

Instead, turn right and walk up the heathery slope alongside the forest fence. It is best to walk some distance from the fence to avoid rutted ground and cross an area of more uniform heather on Tormusk. Drift further and further away from the fence to gain height, crossing more hummocky and awkward ground on Cnoc Shieveina. There are channels of squelchy sphagnum moss to be crossed, and no trodden paths anywhere. Look out for a small cairn overlooking a broad moorland gap. Descend to cross the gap, which proves to be quite richly vegetated. A fence also needs to be crossed, then any route can be chosen up the broad, heathery slopes of Cnoc a' Chapuill.

Clear weather is a distinct advantage on this broad, pathless moorland. There is nothing to mark the 419m summit of Cnoc a' Chapuill and the moorland slopes spread in all directions. There are distant views of the jagged peaks of northern Arran, while closer to hand across Glenscorrodale is Tighvein and more extensive moorlands. Head roughly north-east or even eastwards along the hummocky moorland crest, but keep well above the forested slopes of Glenscorrodale. When a fence is reached, cross it and turn right to follow it.

The fence runs alongside a young forest for a short while, then it turns right and zig-zags on the moorland slope. There is a climb onto a moorland hump, then a swing to the left before a descent which runs alongside another part of the young forest. The fence runs straight down to the top of the Ross Road. Turn left a short way to join the road, then turn right to cross a cattle grid. The rest of the route is simply a matter of following the road back down to Glenscorrodale. The road runs through forest most of the way, but there are views along the length of the glen. Just after a derelict building is noticed on the left, the road twists and turns downhill.

A more level stretch of road returns to the farm of Glenscorrodale.

Glenscorrodale
It is said that a giant called Scorrie lived in the glen - hence the name Glenscorrodale. The only road is the Ross Road, which was constructed in 1821. Its construction involved tenants either giving six days of work towards the project, or making a payment towards the work. Afterwards, tenants were obliged to give three days of work towards its maintenance, or towards the later building of bridges.

WALK 17

Shiskine & Clauchan Glen

There is a varied circular walk available from Shiskine which includes a number of fairly clear paths and tracks. The route runs up through Clauchan Glen, climbs through the forest, takes in some fine heather moorlands and a scenic loch, then descends through forest and runs down through farmland. The walk starts and finishes on the String Road, which was surveyed and designed by Thomas Telford, linking Blackwaterfoot and Brodick. There is accommodation available in Shiskine, but for other services it is necessary to travel to Blackwaterfoot or further afield.

The Route

Distance:	6¹/₂ miles (11km)
Start:	Shiskine, grid ref 913299.
Terrain:	Mostly good tracks and paths, but some rugged moorland walking too.

Find somewhere to park in Shiskine, then start walking along the String Road in the direction of Brodick. After leaving the village, the road crosses a bridge over the Black Water and passes Bridgend Cottages at the foot of Clauchan Glen. Turn right up a narrow tarmac road beyond the cottages. The road has a line of leaning beech trees to the left and a burial ground to the right. The tarmac ends at a small parking space beside the burial ground and a gravel track runs uphill between fields and a forest, passing a covered reservoir, to reach a little cottage called Sron na Carriage.

Pass a barrier and follow the track into the forest. A sign reads: "Forest walk via rough path Glenree Farm 4 miles" and the track bends as it climbs. After a straight stretch, look out for a grassy track heading off to the right. There is a marker post indicating Glenree and a white direction arrow. The track is fringed with heather,

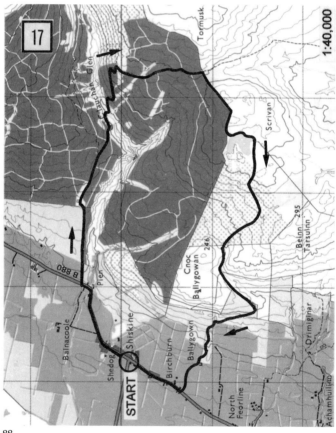

bushes and forest trees, and it drops down to a bouldery ford over the Black Water in Clauchan Glen. The grassy track zig-zags up from the ford, still with heathery banks and occasional peeps through the trees into the glen. There is a broad slope of heather at a higher level, where another marker post for Glenree stands on a bend. There is a muddy stretch, then the track crosses a small burn. There is a slight descent before a gentle ascent to the edge of the forest. Cross a stile beside a gate and turn right.

Follow the forest fence across a heathery gap and up onto the slopes of Scrivan. It is best to walk well away from the fence to avoid rutted ground and cross a more uniform slope of heather. Note a small, tumbled stone shelter while crossing a heathery hump. Views stretch beyond Ard Bheinn to take in some of the larger hills to the north. Turn right around a corner of the forest fence. There is a large patch of squelchy sphagnum moss at this point. A short descent leads to Loch Cnoc an Loch, which has two little islands. Turn left and follow the shoreline, crossing the end of a fence. Look carefully at the moorland slopes to spot the wheel marks left by quad bikes. If these marks prove difficult to spot, then climb to a gentle gap to the west of the loch and look for a cairn, where the track is clearer.

Follow the track down along a ride in a young forest, then turn left to contour across the forested slope. A right turn leads down along another heathery ride, with another slight right turn taking the track down alongside a little burn. There is a gate in the forest fence, from where the track proceeds more clearly through a small valley between Cnoc Ballygowan and Beinn Tarsuinn.

Follow the track through the valley, and cross the little burn a couple of times. Heather and bracken give way to more grassy ground when the track passes through a gate. Follow a fence onwards to reach another gate, where the track swings sharply right. As the track cuts down across the slope, it is sometimes flanked by gorse bushes and views extend across Blackwaterfoot and Machrie. Go through another gate beside a line of beech trees and turn left. The track bends right and left on the way down to the farm of Ballygown, passing through two more gates before reaching the farmyard. Follow the farm access track off to the right to descend to the road. Turn right along the road to walk back through the village of Shiskine. Pass the Church of Scotland and Shiskine Primary School. There are a number of houses and a handful of B&Bs.

Shiskine
The name Shiskine refers to marshy ground, yet there is an expanse of good farmland in the area. There is a story relating that St. Las brought Christianity to Shiskine and that his remains were interred in Clauchan Glen. There is also a tradition that a pilgrimage path ran from Shiskine, up through Clauchan Glen, over to Lamlash and so by ferry to Holy Isle. Up until the 1930s Shiskine was a very industrious village, with a number of shops and businesses, but now it is a quiet place with only a handful of B&Bs, a surgery and an outdoor activity centre.

WALK 18
Ballymichael & Ard Bheinn

Beinn Bhreac and Ard Bheinn are rough and pathless hills rising east of the String Road at Ballymichael. Access is most easily gained via the forest track in Clauchan Glen, but after that the walking is rough and tough. Without trodden paths, there are no easy ways over the two summits, and in misty weather accurate navigation is essential. In order to make a complete circular walk, a stretch of the String Road, surveyed and designed by Thomas Telford, is followed through Ballymichael. There is also the chance to include a tour of the Balmichael Visitor Centre at the start or finish of the walk.

The Route
Distance:	8 miles (13km)
Start:	Balmichael Visitor Centre, grid ref 925315.
Terrain:	A forest track and path, otherwise rugged, pathless moorland needing careful navigation in mist.

There is hardly any room to park beside the road around Ballymichael. The car park at the Balmichael Visitor Centre is for patrons only, but permission could be sought there. Anyone arriving by bus will of course have no parking problems. Follow the road away from Balmichael Visitor Centre as if heading for Shiskine. Turn left up a narrow tarmac road before Bridgend Cottages at the foot of Clauchan Glen. This road has a line of leaning beech trees to the left and a burial ground to the right. The tarmac ends at a small

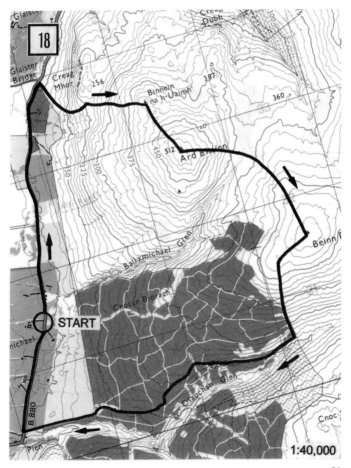

parking space beside the burial ground and a gravel track runs uphill between fields and a forest, passing a covered reservoir, to reach a little cottage called Sron na Carriage.

Pass a barrier and follow the track into the forest. A sign reads: "Forest walk via rough path Glenree Farm 4 miles" and the track bends as it climbs. After a straight stretch, the grassy track marked for Glenree heads off to the right. For this walk, however, keep to the gravel track as it climbs further uphill. When there is a sharp bend to the left, turn right instead, following an older, grassier forest track as it winds uphill past a small quarry. The old track cuts out a loop of the newer track, which is rejoined at a higher level. Turn right to continue ascending gently, reaching the top of the track beside another small quarry. The track begins to descend gently towards the Black Water in Clauchan Glen. Don't go all the way down to the river, as the vegetation cover is too dense and awkward. Look instead for a gravel ramp rising to the left, giving access to a rugged forest ride. Forge a way along the ride to reach the edge of the forest, step over the forest fence, then turn left to walk uphill.

The vegetation cover on the lower slopes of Beinn Bhreac is remarkably varied, comprising bracken, grass, heather, brambles and a host of flowering plants. This makes the ascent interesting, but also rather difficult, and it is best to walk some distance from the line of the forest fence. When a corner of the forest fence is reached, bear slightly to the right and climb straight up the open slope. There is tough heather cover, broken by a few areas of boulders. At a higher level the gradient eases and there is mixed grass and heather cover. Cross a fence and walk along a broad shoulder where there is a pool, then make the final ascent to the broad summit of Beinn Bhreac. There is a stony cairn at 510m situated amid low heathery peat hags. Views northwards stretch from Ard Bheinn and the Pirnmill Hills to Beinn Nuis, Glen Rosa and Goat Fell. In a southerly arc are Holy Isle, Tighvein, Ailsa Craig, Antrim and Kintyre, with Jura beyond.

Descend roughly northwards from the broad moorland summit of Beinn Bhreac, down a gentle slope of heather, grass and low peat hags. The ground becomes steeper and it is best to drift to the left towards a broad gap. A few boulders and rock outcrops are passed, then a broad gap proves to be squelchy with sphagnum moss. Once across the gap, begin climbing fairly steeply on the slopes of Ard

The summit of Beinn Bhreac remains clear of low cloud

Bheinn. Again, it is best to drift a little more to the left. The ground becomes predominantly heathery and there are some boulders and rocky outcrops to pass. The summit bears a trig point at 512m inside a circular stone shelter. There is also a cairn nearby.

Descend roughly northwards from the top of Ard Bheinn, then make another slight drift to the left. The aim is to pick up and follow a broad, hummocky ridge which ends in a dome bearing a cairn. This is Binnein na h-Uaimh and the underlying rock is a bouldery conglomerate. Head westwards to start the descent, then look carefully down the slope to avoid steep ground or rocky outcrops. It is possible to pick a way down steep heathery ground, drifting to the right to enter a little valley behind the hump of Creag Mhor. The upper floor of the valley is a bit wet and bears bog myrtle.

The final part of the descent is quite short, but it is very tough underfoot and needs special care. Stay on the northern side of the Allt nan Dris, away from both the Derneneach Stone Quarry and the forest which can be seen below. Heather gives way to areas of bracken and boulders, which needs to be taken slowly and carefully. At a lower level, there is an ankle-wrenching slope of tussocky grass and more bracken. Aim to reach the String Road to the right of the forest. There is a fence to cross near a road junction, where there is also a fine red sandstone pillar box.

Turn left along the String Road and walk between the forest and a series of fields. Pass the access roads for the Derneneach Stone Quarry and Derneneach Farm. The road is then flanked on both sides by fields. After passing Bridge Farm, which is to the left of the road, the Balmichael Visitor Centre is off to the right of the road.

Balmichael Visitor Centre

Based on a former farm complex, the Balmichael Visitor Centre includes a number of attractions. The Arran Motor Museum is housed in the corner of a courtyard. It is dedicated to the history of family motoring. The Old Mill Coffee House serves snacks and refreshments. There are craft and antique shops around a courtyard. For children, there is an adventure playground, motorised quad biking, and in case of rain, an Indoor Playbarn.

WALK 19
The String & Beinn Bhreac

There are wild, empty moorlands and hills to the south of the String Road. Farmland and forestry makes access difficult in places, but this particular walk has access via a rugged forest path in Glen Craigag. Practically the whole walk is over rough, tough, pathless hill and moorland slopes, with the circuit being closed by a road walk at the end. Parking is very limited beside the String Road, but there are regular bus services back and forth. The route takes in three summits - A' Chruach, Beinn Bhreac and Ard Bheinn - which are all arranged in a circuit around Glen Craigag.

The Route

Distance:	7$^{1}/_{2}$ miles (12km)
Start:	Glenloig, String Road, grid ref 946351.
Terrain:	A forest path and rugged, pathless moorlands needing careful navigation in mist.

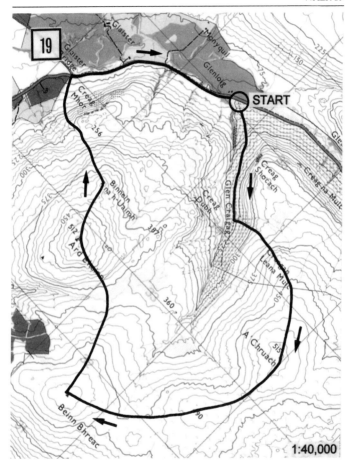

Parking on the String Road is quite limited, but there is a space opposite the farm called Glenloig, which is the last farm when travelling up the String Road towards Brodick. Just a short distance further away from the farm is a gateway and a Forestry Commission sign reading "Glenloig". The whole of the northern side of Glen Craigag has been forested, but there is a single ride through it which

95

has been left unplanted. While this ride bears a vague, trodden path, it is also covered in bracken, tussocky grass and heather, making it a tough walk. When the path leaves the roadside at the gateway, it follows a fence through the bracken, then rises through the forest ride. Follow the ride until there is an awkward crossing of a little burn. At the next little burn, reached almost immediately afterwards, it is best to abandon the course of the ride and walk straight uphill.

Again, there is a vaguely trodden path on a slope of bracken, which gives way to steep, pathless heather above the forest. As a gentler moorland shoulder is gained, swing more to the right. Some of the higher peaks of northern Arran are seen across the broad moorlands, stretching from Beinn Bharrain to Goat Fell. There is another short, steep climb, punctuated by a few boulders and low outcrops of rock, on the slopes of Creagan Leana Muic. There is a fence to be crossed, then a gentler moorland slope leads onwards and upwards to the summit of A' Chruach. This ascent ends on a broad grass and heather rise bearing a small cairn at 515m. Views stretch from the high peaks of northern Arran to the extensive moorlands of southern Arran, taking in the Ayr and Galloway coasts, Antrim and Kintyre. Islands in view include Cumbrae, Holy Isle, Ailsa Craig and Jura.

Head due southwards in the direction of Ailsa Craig along the broad moorland crest. There is a trace of a path, but not much, and not enough to follow confidently in mist. After crossing the next broad moorland gap, drift to the right to cross a broad, bleak moorland summit of low peat hags at 490m. The next gap on the moorland crest is very broad and gentle, but it is also abundantly boggy and covered in grass, sphagnum moss and peat hags. It is best avoided altogether by keeping to the northern slope of the moors, overlooking Glen Craigag. After passing somewhat below the gap, a firmer ascent can be made on the slopes of Beinn Bhreac. There is a stony cairn on top at 510m situated amid low heathery peat hags.

Descend roughly northwards from the broad moorland summit of Beinn Bhreac, down a gentle slope of heather, grass and low peat hags. The ground becomes steeper and it is best to drift to the left towards a broad gap. A few boulders and rock outcrops are passed, then a broad gap proves to be squelchy with sphagnum moss. Once across the gap, begin climbing fairly steeply on the slopes of Ard Bheinn. Again, it is best to drift a little more to the left. The ground becomes predominantly heathery and there are some boulders and rocky outcrops to pass. The summit bears a trig point at 512m inside a circular stone shelter. There is also a cairn nearby. Views stretch across the desolate moorlands of southern Arran, as well as northwards to the jagged peaks of the higher mountains.

Descend roughly northwards from the top of Ard Bheinn, then make another slight drift to the left. The aim is to pick up and follow a broad, hummocky ridge which ends in a dome bearing a cairn. This is Binnein na h-Uaimh and the underlying rock is a bouldery conglomerate. Head westwards to start the descent, then look carefully down the slope to avoid steep ground or rocky outcrops. It is possible to pick a way down steep heathery ground, drifting to the right to enter a little valley behind the hump of Creag Mhor. The upper floor of the valley is a bit wet and bears bog myrtle.

The final part of the descent is quite short, but it is very tough underfoot and needs special care. Stay on the northern side of the Allt nan Dris, away from both the Derneneach Stone Quarry and the forest which can be seen below. Heather gives way to areas of bracken and boulders, which needs to be taken slowly and carefully. At a lower level, there is an ankle-wrenching slope of tussocky grass and more bracken. Aim to reach the String Road just to the right of the forest. There is a fence to cross near a road junction, where there is also a fine red sandstone pillar box.

Turn right along the String Road from the junction. Walk around the rugged slopes at the foot of Creag Mhor, passing the access tracks for Glaister and Monyquil farms. Immediately after crossing a bridge at the foot of Glen Craigag the circuit is brought to a close at Glenloig.

The String
The String Road, or B880, cuts the Isle of Arran in half. To the north are the high, jagged, rocky mountain peaks, surrounded by a tall deer fence. To the south are lower hills, extensive moorlands and forests. The String Road was surveyed by Thomas Telford in 1817, though traces of earlier paths and tracks can still be distinguished on parallel courses on the adjacent slopes.

WALK 20

Blackwaterfoot & King's Cave

One of the most popular easy walks on the Isle of Arran takes in the King's Cave. There are two paths allowing easy approaches; one from Blackwaterfoot and the other from Machrie Moor. These paths can be combined so that a route from Blackwaterfoot to the King's Cave and onwards to Machrie Moor is possible. Both ends of the walk have car parks and bus services, but the only easy way to turn the walk into a circuit involves following the road back to Blackwaterfoot. Paths shown on maps of Machrie Moor are quite overgrown and difficult to follow, and so are not recommended. Before setting off, walkers should note that there is a gate across the mouth of the King's Cave, protecting the cave from vandalism and misuse. Anyone who wants to explore deep inside the cave will need to obtain a key in advance. Contact the Tourist Information Centre at Brodick for details of the Keyholder.

The Route

Distance:	6 miles (10km)
Start:	Blackwaterfoot Harbour, grid ref 895282.
Terrain:	Clear paths, tracks and roads, but some of the paths can be wet and muddy.

Start from the car park beside the Kinloch Hotel in Blackwaterfoot and follow the main road across the bridge overlooking the tiny harbour. On the other side of the bridge is a little waterfall. Continue along the main coastal road, then switch to a minor road signposted on the left for a golf course. This road reaches a private car park for the Shiskine Golf and Tennis Club and the Blackwaterfoot Bowling Club. There is a public footpath sign indicating the way to the King's Cave. Follow a broad coastal track, noting a couple of rocky dykes standing above the level of the sandy beach. A line of low dunes are covered in spiky marram grass. The track turns inland and reaches the piers of a gateway in a fence. Turn left at this point, where there is another sign for the King's Cave. Follow the fence until signs indicate a way up to a gate. A path crosses two fields before a waymark post points to the left, revealing a path zig-zagging down onto a raised beach.

Note the columnar cliffs facing the sea at Doon, covered in plants and flowers safe from grazing sheep. The top of the Doon bears traces of an Iron Age hill fort. Turn right to follow a cobbly, grassy path past an old sea stack now marooned on the raised beach. The rock is exotically encrusted with lichens. The route proceeds

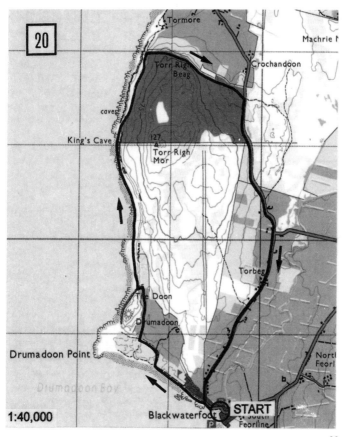

easily on short grass, then climbs as a narrow, rocky path to avoid a bouldery beach walk.

A series of caves are encountered; at least fifteen distinct examples. The first cave is small and choked with brambles. The second is larger, while the third and fourth are separated only by a pillar of rock. There is plenty of headroom for those who want to walk from one to the other. The fifth cave is narrower and is like a passageway leading through to the entrance to the King's Cave, which is itself the sixth in the series. A sign fixed to a decorative set of railings reads: "It has been necessary to restrict access to the cave in order to preserve this important archaeological site which has evidence of human occupation dating back thousands of years. Interested parties can still gain access to the cave. For further information please telephone the Tourist Information Centre at Brodick on 302401." The seventh cave is a narrow slit which can be walked through just beyond the entrance to the King's Cave. The eighth cave is choked with scrub and the ninth is just beyond a short drystone wall. The tenth cave is a step up above the raised beach, while the eleventh is quite low-cut. The twelfth is almost obscured by boulders and it is possible to crawl beneath a low arch to reach the thirteenth. Only consider crawling if wearing old clothes, as the floor of the cave is quite mucky. The fourteenth cave is wet and muddy, while the fifteenth has a pool of water inside.

The path climbs uphill immediately beside the fifteenth cave. It rises from a pebbly beach and can be muddy until it crosses a stile and proceeds through a rocky cut. A clear, broad, earth and stone path runs uphill parallel to the edge of a forest on the slopes of Torr Righ Mor. It runs along the edge of a heathery brow overlooking the sea and the distant hills of Kintyre. The path cuts a corner of the forest when it turns inland, climbing over a rise where benches offer the chance to take a break with views over the gentle farming landscape of Machrie. The path runs gently downhill to cross a burn, then climbs a little inside the forest before dropping to a car park. An information board beside the car park points out the existence of some ancient hut circles nearby, as well as offering notes about the King's Cave and the Machrie Moor Stone Circles.

Walkers who wish to start from this car park will find that the place is signposted in advance for travellers coming either way

Striking columnar cliffs at Drumadoon on the way to King's Cave

along the road. While maps may show paths on nearby Machrie Moor, and the Machrie Stone Circles look deceptively close on the map, there is no easy way to tie everything together in a circular walk. Machrie Moor is rough and boggy and the few paths which cross it are quite overgrown and difficult to follow. A separate walk takes in the Machrie Moor Stone Circles (Walk 21). To return to Blackwaterfoot, the main road is recommended. Turn right to follow it after leaving the forest car park. The road overlooks Machrie Moor and is often flanked by shrubs and scrub. A small sign later announces the scattered settlement of Torbeg. Shiskine Free Church of Scotland stands to the right, while to the left at a road junction is a memorial to a former minister - Rev Archibald Nichol. The main road continues straight on for Blackwaterfoot, climbing uphill and passing a small school, then running gradually downhill, passing the Greannan B&B and a number of bungalows. Turn left at the bottom to follow the coastal road into Blackwaterfoot. Most of the facilities in the village are concentrated on both sides of the tiny harbour.

Blackwaterfoot

Originally, Blackwaterfoot was a small, close-knit community with a few houses positioned around the tiny harbour. There was a massive burial cairn above the village, but this was gradually reduced and plundered for building material. In 1900 a bronze dagger with gold decoration was retrieved from the centre of the cairn. Features and facilities from north to south in the village include the Harbour Shop (newsagents, hardware, fancy goods), butcher, then the waterfall, bridge and tiny harbour. Across the bridge are toilets, a car park and the large Kinloch Hotel and leisure centre. Going uphill is the Salon, Morvern Guest House (in an old bank), Post Office and grocery, and cycle hire. The Blackwaterfoot Hotel faces a garage on the way out of the village, with the Cairnhouse Riding Centre a short way beyond.

King's Cave

History and mystery surround the caves between Blackwaterfoot and Machrie. There are some interesting carvings from the early Christian and Pictish periods, and the caves are thought to have been used by early Christian voyagers and missionaries among the islands. Some legends relate that Robert the Bruce hid in the King's Cave (hence the name) and had his legendary encounter with the spider, or waited for a signal beacon to be lit, but there is no evidence to support either tale. It is, however, quite possible that he used the cave briefly while fleeing to Rathlin Island off the Antrim coast in 1306.

Machrie Moor

The farming landscape of Machrie Moor has a very long history. Hut circles exist where the King's Cave path reaches the forest car park. A series of famous stone circles are located nearby. The hut circles date from Late Neolithic to Early Bronze Age. The stone circles on Machrie Moor are reckoned to be around 4000 years old. The existence of these remains and monuments indicates that a series of settled, agricultural communities lived in this area. (See also Walk 21.)

Three tall standing stones on Machrie Moor with Goat Fell beyond

WALK 21

Machrie Moor Stone Circles

One of the easiest and most interesting walks on the Isle of Arran is the one to the Machrie Moor Stone Circles. This could be accomplished in almost any weather, but in fine weather there is a chance to experience the spaciousness of the site. A number of stone circles and stone uprights can be inspected from a gravel track and moorland path. All around are ranged some of the highest and most rugged mountains on the island, which make a superb backdrop for photographers wanting to capture the spirit of the place. The only drawbacks are that parking can be very tight and the area can be busy with other visitors. However, walking there in the quiet times of the year can be a good idea.

The Route

Distance:	2 miles (3km)
Start:	Near Machrie Water, grid ref 895330.
Terrain:	A good track ending with moorlands which can be wet underfoot.

This short, easy walk starts beside the main road near Machrie Water. There is a sign beside the road reading "Machrie Moor Stone Circles 1 mile". Parking beside the road is very tight, but there is a little more space roughly opposite. Leave the road at a gate and stile and follow the track across a field to another gate and stile. The track rises and bends right and left. At another gate and stile is the Moss Farm Road Stone Circle in a fenced enclosure. The track continues clearly over a moorland rise, and there are small standing stones to right and left before the next gate and stile. Shortly afterwards, pass through a gateway to find a stone circle to the right, above the derelict buildings of Moss Farm. Cross another stile and study two information boards relating to Machrie Moor.

There is a stone circle to the right of the information boards, and a narrow moorland path leads to three tall upright stones. Beyond these are two more stone circles. Retracing steps a little, but branching off to the right, is a tall, solitary upright stone. All around this

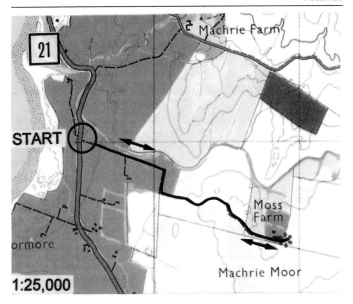

moorland setting are ranged the peaks of Beinn Bharrain, Sail Chalmadale, Beinn Nuis, Goat Fell and Ard Bheinn. When the stone circles and uprights have been thoroughly investigated, simply retrace steps from Moss Farm to the main road along the gravel track.

Machrie Moor Stone Circles
Machrie Moor is a well preserved Neolithic and Bronze Age ritual landscape. The Moss Farm Road Stone Circle is unusual, as it may actually be a kerbed cairn, or the cairn was constructed before the stone circle. Apart from stone circles and stone uprights, the area around Machrie Moor is dotted with hut circles, indicating that people lived in a settled, agricultural community. There must have been a high degree of community involvement for them to have raised so many fine structures and monuments.

WALK 22

Dougarie & Beinn Nuis

Beinn Nuis is almost always climbed from Glen Rosa, and that is the way its paths are trodden. Its rugged form dominates Glen Iorsa, but few walkers attempt a summit bid from that direction and there are very few trodden paths on the way. The route described here uses the access track leading to Loch Iorsa, then takes to the desolate uplands, reaching Beinn Nuis by way of a fine, bouldery ridge. There is a chance to walk around the bouldery bowl of Coire Nuis and head across empty moorlands to reach Loch Nuis. While steps could be retraced through Glen Iorsa, another ending can be contemplated, following a forest fence across boggy moorland slopes to descend to Machrie. A short road walk leads back from Machrie to Dougarie. Then again, there is another alternative route. Walkers can climb above Glen Iorsa, then rather than head for the distant Beinn Nuis, they can simply turn right and follow the forest fence straight to Machrie. A glance at the map illustrates the choice of routes available.

The Route

Distance:	12 miles (19km)
Start:	Dougarie, grid ref 882370.
Terrain:	Some tracks, but mostly pathless moorlands and mountain, boggy and bouldery in many places.

There is only a small space to park cars at Dougarie, beside a white hut on the southern side of the bridge. Set off walking towards Dougarie Lodge, which is seen briefly on both sides of the bridge spanning Iorsa Water at its confluence with the sea. The access road for Dougarie Lodge is marked as private, with another sign indicating that a footpath is available further along the road. Walk along the road and round a bend, then take a track on the right, which is signposted as a footpath. Gravel gives way to concrete as this track climbs and bends left, then another sign indicates the footpath heading off to the right.

Follow this narrow path up a banking and cross over a wall. The path follows the wall through a couple of fields, crossing two fences. Continue through a small wood and cross another fence, then follow the path across a slope of bracken. The path dips down to cross a stile over another fence, then joins a track. Cross either a concrete ford or a footbridge over the Allt na h' Airidhe and keep walking along the track in view of Iorsa Water. The river is broad and bouldery and is the biggest river on the island. It cuts through masses of glacial rubble, whose ill-bedded layers can be seen alongside the track. Go through a gate in a tall deer fence, then either cross another concrete ford, or look upstream for a footbridge spanning the river at the foot of Glen Scaftigill. The track continues across a slope of tussocky grass, heather and bog myrtle to reach the foot of Loch Iorsa, where there is a tiny boathouse.

A grassy and often boggy track pushes further up into Glen Iorsa, running alongside the shore of Loch Iorsa and continuing beside Iorsa Water. There is bog myrtle amid the grass and heather. Look out for a couple of wooden posts - one on either side of the river - which mark an old ford. The water would need to be very low indeed before there was any chance of crossing dry-shod. A little further upstream, however, are shoals of reddish gravel where the channel is braided and there is a greater chance of crossing without getting wet feet. In times of spate and high water, this walk may be impossible to continue, and walkers may need to switch to the Sail Chalmadale route (Walk 23) instead.

If Iorsa Water can be safely forded, then look uphill to spot a bracken filled groove running from top to bottom on the southern flank of the glen. Avoid the areas of bracken and keep to the left of the groove while climbing uphill. There is tussocky grass, heather and bog myrtle, with a few trees noticed at a higher level. Views open up both ways along the bleak and barren glen. After passing the trees, the gradient eases a little and a handful of small, ancient cairns are passed. Later, a forest is seen on the horizon ahead. Begin to drift to the left across the slope, picking up any useful animal paths along the way. Cross over the Allt Airidh Mhuirich and rise over a huge, boggy hump of moorland. Off to the right is Loch Nuis and a couple of rashes of boulders are passed on the grass and heather moorland on the way towards the towering form of Beinn Nuis.

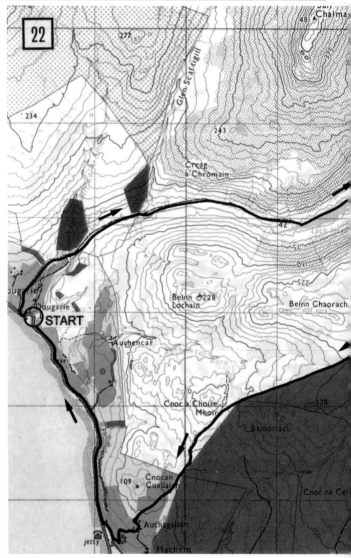

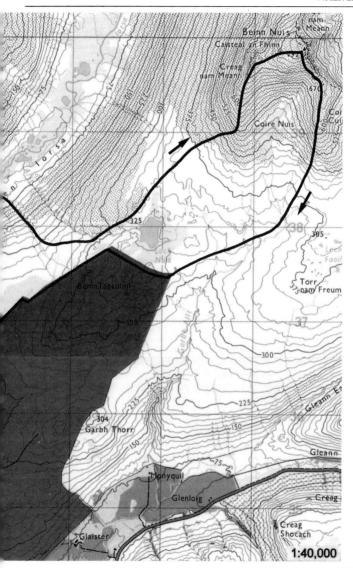

The ground steepens and it is best to keep to the right to join a boulder-strewn ridge. The rounded ridge is mostly heather studded with boulders, with views extending from Kintyre and Antrim to Holy Isle and the Ayrshire coast. The climb up the rounded ridge proves relatively easy after the tussocky moors. The ground becomes predominantly bouldery, then rather gritty, then a fine, blocky ridge of granite develops, with good views across Glen Iorsa to the Pirnmill Hills. Cross a little gap, then climb up a steep slope of short heather and boulders. After passing a wrinkly little tor of granite, a gentler, grassier, less bouldery slope leads to the top of Beinn Nuis. The bouldery summit bears a little cairn at 792m and features good views around Glen Rosa.

Turn right to follow a path away from the summit cairn. This path runs down a steep, rocky slope beside a precipitous cliff. When a gentle gap is reached, the path heads off towards Glen Rosa, but this walk turns right to cross a gentle summit of short grass, heather, low outcrops and boulders. The end of this little crest steepens abruptly and falls towards a broad, boggy moorland drained by the Garbh Allt. In clear weather, the lonely moorland pool of Loch Nuis will be in view. There are all sorts of vague paths on the moorlands below, but none of them can be followed for any great distance. Aim to reach the course of the Garbh Allt, crossing it to walk on the right-hand side. Loch Nuis will have passed from sight, but aim instead for the corner of a forest seen ahead on a rise of moorland. The grass and heather can be tussocky in places and makes for a rough passage.

The forest fence is the key to the long descent from the moors. Turn right to follow the fence uphill across a rise of moorland on Beinn Tarsuinn. Loch Nuis comes into view again, with Beinn Nuis well framed beyond. The fence runs downhill a short way, then there is a left turn around a corner. Continue following the fence downhill, then across a more level area with many boggy patches. There is a rise and fall as the hump of Beinn Chaorach is passed. The fence descends to cross a burn, then rises a little, then descends again. Bracken patches impede progress a little near the hump of Cnoc a' Choire Mhoir.

Look out for an old track just to the right of the forest fence. Pick up this line and follow it through a gate in a tall deer fence. The grassy track can be traced across fields, crossing the gentle slopes of Cnocan Cuallaich. The track runs down towards a huddle of farm buildings at Auchagallon. Turn left through a gate and follow the clearest, broadest gravel track which zig-zags downhill. The lowest zig-zag turns around a small enclosure where Auchagallon Stone Circle is located. Continue down to the road. This is a minor road, with the main coastal road lying just beyond. Turn right along both roads, walking from the Machrie Garage back towards Dougarie. A scrub-covered sandstone cliff along the way features a handful of caves. A red sandstone house flanked by trees is passed. A signposted turning offers a detour a short way uphill to the Old Byre Showroom and the Auchencar Druid Stone. Walkers could follow a grassy strip beside the coastal road on the final stretch back to Dougarie.

Auchagallon Stone Circle
Although often referred to as a stone circle, the site at Auchagallon is actually a kerbed cairn. The remaining upright slabs lie inwards around an ancient grassy cairn, probably dating back 4000 years. Excavations carried out in the 19th century revealed a cist burial in the middle of the cairn. Kerbed cairns are thought to have been constructed as burial places for important people, creating a site which would impress visitors and remind them of the importance of the person within. The nearby Moss Farm Road Stone Circle on Machrie Moor may be of the same type of construction.

Auchencar Druid Stone
Situated in a large field off the access road for Auchencar, the Druid Stone is the tallest standing stone on the Isle of Arran. The stone itself is a blade of rock, which looks tall and broad from one side, yet tall and narrow from the other. Its isolation in a broad field removed from habitation, yet within view of the mountains, adds to its impressiveness.

Old Byre Showroom
The Old Byre Showroom is signposted from the access road for Auchencar. Sheepskins, leather goods, woollens and other items of clothing are sold, some with designer labels.

WALK 23
Dougarie & Sail Chalmadale

When the high mountains around Glen Iorsa are shrouded in cloud, it is often the case that Sail Chalmadale will be clear. A combination of its lower height and proximity to its loftier neighbours gives it some measure of protection from low cloud. The access track running to Loch Iorsa from Dougarie is an obvious way towards Sail Chalmadale, and the mountain can be climbed gradually in a sort of spiral route from the glen. A descent can be made back towards the main track in the glen, finishing with a walk back to the main road at Dougarie. Despite its low stature, Sail Chalmadale offers a fine, rugged upland walk.

The Route

Distance:	10 miles (16km)
Start:	Dougarie, grid ref 882370.
Terrain:	Gravel and boggy tracks, as well as pathless uplands, boggy and rocky ground.

There is only a small space to park cars at Dougarie, beside a white hut on the south side of the bridge. Set off walking towards Dougarie Lodge, which is seen briefly on both sides of the bridge spanning Iorsa Water at its confluence with the sea. The access road for Dougarie Lodge is marked as private, with another sign indicating that a footpath is available further along the road. Walk along the road and round a bend, then take a track on the right, which is signposted as a footpath. Gravel gives way to concrete as this track climbs and bends left, then another sign indicates the footpath heading off to the right.

Follow this narrow path up a banking and cross over a wall. The path follows the wall through a couple of fields, crossing two fences. Continue through a small wood and cross another fence, then follow the path across a slope of bracken. The path dips down to cross a stile over another fence, then joins a track. Cross either a concrete ford or a footbridge over the Allt na h' Airidhe and keep

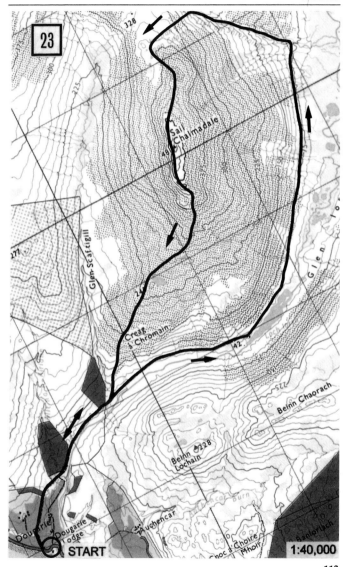

1:40,000

113

walking along the track in view of Iorsa Water. The river is broad and bouldery and is the biggest river on the island. It cuts through masses of glacial rubble, whose ill-bedded layers can be seen alongside the track. Go through a gate in a tall deer fence, then either cross another concrete ford, or look upstream for a footbridge spanning the river at the foot of Glen Scaftigill. The track continues across a slope of tussocky grass, heather and bog myrtle to reach the foot of Loch Iorsa, where there is a tiny boathouse.

A grassy and often boggy track pushes further up into Glen Iorsa, running alongside the shore of Loch Iorsa and continuing beside Iorsa Water. The track has been blazed by quad bikes being ridden into the glen and the route is braided in places. The route avoids the broad and boggy floor of the glen, and sticks instead to the lower slopes of Sail Chalmadale. Follow this track as far as the Allt Tigh an Shiorraim, crossing both channels of the bouldery burn. Turn left to trace the burn upstream, but also keep well to the right of it.

Aim to walk along the top of a high banking overlooking the bouldery watercourse, where a vague path can be traced through the grass and heather, weaving past scattered boulders. At a higher level all traces of the path are lost, but it is still a good idea to keep to a rugged moorland shelf above the burn. Later, choose any point at which to ford the burn. Obviously, the higher the burn is forded, the less climbing there is on the slope opposite.

The broad crest of Sail Chalmadale is bouldery, with shorter grass and heather, as well as exposed gritty soil in places. Walk along the crest by turning left, passing to the left side of the little Lochan nan Cnamh. Walk up a slope of rocky ribs and low boulders, crossing a rugged, domed summit. Cross over a little gap, then climb another bouldery slope at a fairly gentle gradient. There is a cairn on top of Sail Chalmadale at 481m, surrounded by boulders poking up from short heather. The view includes a host of higher summits arranged around Glen Iorsa. Looking seawards, however, it is possible to spot Jura, Kintyre, Antrim and even Ailsa Craig over a shoulder of broad moorland.

There is a narrow path trodden away from the summit, running roughly southwards, but it soon vanishes. Keep walking onwards until the lower parts of the ridge can be seen, bearing two small lochans. Start to drift to the left to descend more steeply, to avoid unseen sloping slabs of granite. Keep well to the left of the two lochans, and they pass from sight on the descent. However, once more gentle slopes have been gained, turn right and pass to the right of both lochans on the broad moorland shoulder. Another vague track has been made by quad bikes in this direction, and it should be possible to trace the line further downhill. The lower slopes, around Creag a' Chromain, are composed of tussocky grass, heather, bracken and bog myrtle.

When the main track running through Glen Iorsa is gained, it is simply a matter of turning right and retracing the earlier steps of the day. Cross either the concrete ford or footbridge and pass through the gate in the tall deer fence. Follow the track to the next ford and footbridge. A small sign indicates the footpath to the road off to the right. Cross the slope of bracken, walk through the small wood and two fields, then follow the track back to the main coastal road. Turn left to pass in front of Dougarie Lodge and cross the bridge over Iorsa Water.

Dougarie Lodge
The attractive whitewashed building of Dougarie Lodge was built towards the end of the 19th century as a shooting lodge. Although the red deer population on Arran had almost been wiped out by the beginning of the 19th century, there was considerable restocking and the northern half of the island was made into a deer forest secured by a tall deer fence. At one time the exterior of Dougarie Lodge was covered in antlers, but now the building is simply whitewashed. There is no public access to the lodge, and walkers are directed along a footpath which keeps away from the building.

WALK 24
Circuit of Glen Iorsa

One of the toughest and most remote day's walks on the Isle of Arran must be the circuit around Glen Iorsa. This broad, bleak and boggy glen slices through northern Arran and is without any

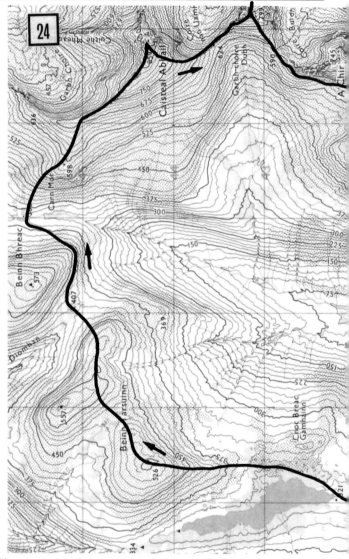

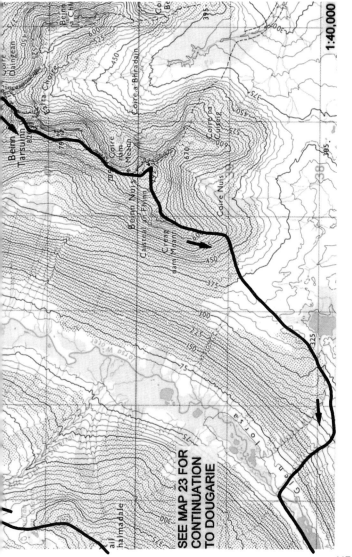

1:40,000

SEE MAP 23 FOR
CONTINUATION
TO DOUGARIE

habitations apart from Dougarie Lodge beside the sea. The route takes in Sail Chalmadale, Loch Tanna, Beinn Tarsuinn and Loch na Davie. There are ascents of Caisteal Abhail and the rocky Cir Mhor. By-passing the rocky ridge of A' Chir, the route climbs over Beinn Tarsuinn and Beinn Nuis before making a long descent towards Loch Iorsa. Paths are few and vague for the first half of the walk, though they are much clearer over the higher, rockier mountains. Walkers who attempt this long and hard walk should have an escape plan in mind. While a descent into Glen Iorsa is possible from many points, it could involve crossing very rugged, pathless terrain. Descents into other glens could be preferable.

The Route

Distance:	20 miles (32km)
Start:	Dougarie, grid ref 882370.
Terrain:	Some good ridge paths and vague moorland paths, but often rocky, boggy terrain.

There is only a small space to park cars at Dougarie, beside a white hut on the south side of the bridge. Set off walking towards Dougarie Lodge, which is seen briefly on both sides of the bridge spanning Iorsa Water at its confluence with the sea. The access road for Dougarie Lodge is marked as private, with another sign indicating that a footpath is available further along the road. Walk along the road and round a bend, then take a track on the right, which is signposted as a footpath. Gravel gives way to concrete as this track climbs and bends left, then another sign indicates the footpath heading off to the right.

Follow this narrow path up a banking and cross over a wall. The path follows the wall through a couple of fields, crossing two fences. Continue through a small wood and cross another fence, then follow the path across a slope of bracken. The path dips down to cross a stile over another fence, then joins a track. Cross either a concrete ford or a footbridge over the Allt na h' Airidhe and keep walking along the track in view of Iorsa Water. The river is broad and bouldery and is the biggest river on the island. It cuts through masses of glacial rubble, whose ill-bedded layers can be seen alongside the track. Go through a gate in a tall deer fence, then either cross another concrete ford, or look upstream for a footbridge spanning the river at the foot of Glen Scaftigill.

Turn left to pick up a vague track made by quad bikes on the lower slopes of Sail Chalmadale. The track crosses tussocky grass, heather, bracken and bog myrtle around Creag a' Chromain and climbs uphill to pass two little lochans on a moorland shoulder. The rugged top of Sail Chalmadale rises ahead, but there are steep slopes of granite in view. Keep well to the right to outflank these and climb more steeply uphill. The summit crest is much gentler and there is even a vague path which leads across short heather and boulders to the summit cairn at 481m. There is a chance to observe the whole of the route around Glen Iorsa, from Loch Tanna to Caisteal Abhail and Beinn Nuis. It is a daunting prospect after the tough ascent of lowly Sail Chalmadale.

Continue walking along the crest of Sail Chalmadale, walking down a bouldery slope to cross a little gap. Walk over the next rugged, domed summit and cross areas of rocky ribs and boulders on the short descent towards Lochan nan Cnamh. Pass the lochan on its right side and continue across a broader moorland slope which is bouldery in some parts and clothed in tussocky grass and heather in other parts. Aim for the outflow from Loch Tanna, crossing the Allt Tigh an Shiorraim to walk along the eastern shore of the loch.

Following the shore of the loch is rather too rough and wet, so it is better to drift away from the shore and head northwards towards the hill. The moorland slope can be boggy and rocky in places, and as the ground steepens there is prostrate juniper couched amid the rock and heather. The first part of Beinn Tarsuinn is broad, gritty, bouldery and features some low outcrops of granite. The only cairn is a small construction just off the 526m summit. Continue across the summit, down to a broad, boggy gap, then climb uphill towards a slightly higher part of Beinn Tarsuinn. Don't go to the summit, but drift to the right and drop gently onto a bouldery shoulder. Next, bear left and make a steep and bouldery descent from the crest of Beinn Tarsuinn to a broad gap of boggy ground and stony patches.

Towering above is the awesomely bouldery Beinn Bhreac, but there is no need to climb to the top. Instead, turn right along a vague and stony path, cutting around a shoulder of the hill and dropping gently towards Loch na Davie. Cross in front of the little lough on boggy ground, then reach a firmer footing on the steep and bouldery slopes of Carn Mor. This is a major turning point in the route, but there is much effort to be expended on the ascent and a break of slope at 598m proves welcome. Continue climbing up the pathless slope to emerge suddenly on a fine, sweeping, curved ridge overlooking the Garbh Choire. This ridge is often referred to as the "Dress Circle". A right turn up the ridge leads eventually to the summit of Caisteal Abhail at 859m. There are a handful of granite tors on the summit which have the appearance of ruined castles.

Pick a way roughly southwards down from the summit and walk around the rough and rocky Coire nan Uamh. The next summit in line is the impressively steep and rocky pyramid of Cir Mhor. Walkers should feel drawn to make the climb to the 799m summit, but the walk is already well advanced and some may be having problems. Dissipating energy and dwindling daylight are to be guarded against, and it is only fair to point out that there is a path cutting across the Glen Iorsa flank of Cir Mhor, omitting the rocky summit.

Rising above the next gap are the rocky buttresses of A' Chir, where walkers would normally not tread. The full traverse of the A' Chir ridge is technically a rock climb, with some very exposed moves. Walkers start by climbing along the rocky crest, but should look carefully for a path which ducks off to the right, from some flat slabs on the Glen Iorsa flank of the mountain. This narrow, stony, rocky path sneaks across a rugged slope and passes beneath weeping boilerplate slabs of granite which support only a few little rugs of heather. The path then climbs gradually to the next gap, which is Beallach an Fhir-bhogha.

Towering above Beallach an Fhir-bhogha is Beinn Tarsuinn, whose dark granite buttresses frown on humble walkers - especially on those who are tired and still have a long walk ahead of them. A rocky, bouldery path keeps to the right of the main buttress, and although there are sometimes alternative lines available, all of them involve the use of hands for balance at some point. The lower parts are tougher than the upper parts, and there is even the option of walking beneath a huge boulder at one point. There are twin summits at 826m, both having low outcrops and boulders of granite. A short, bouldery slope leads down to a dip and on the short pull upwards the human profile of the Old Man of Tarsuinn will be seen to the left. A narrow ridge runs downhill, broadens and becomes covered in moss and short grass. Large rounded boulders are passed as the ridge broadens, then a narrow gap is crossed before a short ascent of a steep and bouldery slope leads onto the top of Beinn Nuis. A small cairn sits on the summit at 792m.

Views extend along the length of Glen Iorsa from this final summit, but the coast still seems very distant. Walk westwards to leave, swinging more south-west on a slope of short grass and boulders. Pass to the left of a small wrinkly tor and cross a little gap below. A short ascent is followed by a left turn, tracing a rocky, blocky ridge downhill. The ridge broadens and becomes gritty, then more bouldery and heathery. Below the rounded ridge is an expanse of moorland broken by the shape of Loch Nuis. Head off to the right of the ridge, and cross a moorland rise, keeping to the right of Loch Nuis too. A couple of rashes of boulders are passed on the moorland, and the Allt Airidh Mhuirich can be forded at a point where animal paths converge.

Continue across the moorland slope, losing height gradually and aiming westwards, picking up any narrow paths which seem to be leading that way. Look over the rounded edge into Glen Iorsa and try and spot a handful of ancient grassy cairns. Walking straight downhill from these leads to a bracken filled groove with a few little trees at the top. Keep to the right of this groove to descend a rugged slope into Glen Iorsa. Walk towards Iorsa Water at a point where shoals of reddish gravel can be seen. The water needs to be running fairly low, but it is possible to cross where the channel is braided and the water isn't too deep. Once across, pick up the course of a boggy, grassy track made by quad bikes, and follow this roughly parallel to Loch Iorsa.

At the foot of Loch Iorsa is a tiny boathouse and a gravel track. The gravel track marks firm ground and a safe exit after the endless mountains and bogs of this circuit. Follow the track down the glen to reach the concrete ford and footbridge passed earlier in the day. Simply retrace steps to the main coastal road at Dougarie. Pass through the gate in the tall deer fence. Follow the track to the next ford and footbridge. A small sign indicates the footpath to the road off to the right. Cross the slope of bracken, walk through the small wood and two fields, then follow the track back to the main coastal road. Turn left to pass in front of Dougarie Lodge and cross the bridge over Iorsa Water.

WALK 25
Imachar & Beinn Bharrain

Large blocks of forestry plantations have been established on Ceann Reamhar and Roileag above Whitefarland and Imachar. While not being particularly lovely, they are largely tucked out of sight. They are also served by clear gravel tracks which run fairly close to Beinn Bharrain. The route described here uses forestry tracks on the outward and return journeys and attempts to link them with a high-level walk over the top of Beinn Bharrain. The mountain is surrounded by rugged, largely pathless slopes. The route has been structured to include the lonely Dubh Loch and Loch Tanna, as well as the unfrequented Glen Scaftigill. As some parts are quite rugged, this is a walk for the agile, sure-footed walker who can navigate competently in mist.

The Route

Distance:	12 miles (19km)
Start:	Between Whitefarland and Imachar, grid ref 863414.
Terrain:	Forest tracks and mountain paths, but mostly pathless moorland needing care in mist.

Start on the main coastal road between the farmsteads of Imachar and Whitefarland. There is a track running uphill from the road, flanked by double gates. Parking is not really possible at this point, or for some distance either way along the road, but walkers travelling by bus can simply hop off at this point and start walking. The track climbs across a hillside which is variously vegetated, but mostly covered in grass and bracken. The track zig-zags right and left, passing a prominent mast in a small compound beside a brick hut.

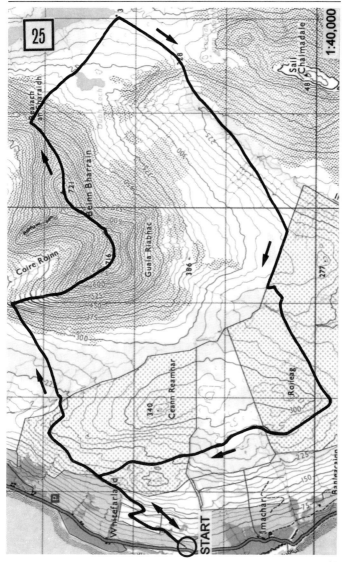

Continue along the track, passing through a gate, then reaching a taller gate in a deer fence surrounding a forest. There is much more heather evident at this point.

Follow the track up through the forest and keep left at a junction of tracks. The track follows a broad, heathery strip through the forest, then bends sharply to the right as it continues to climb. It expires suddenly on a broad, heathery ride. Turn left and follow another short ride downhill to the forest fence. There is no gate, though there is evidence that other people have walked this way. Very thin walkers could squeeze beneath the tall deer fence, while more portly ones could climb at a straining post. Either way, agility is called for and this should be borne in mind before starting the walk.

Head straight towards a burn in a rocky cut outside the forest. Look carefully and a rather narrow, precarious path will be spotted crossing from one side to the other. Pick a way across with care, but note that it may be impassable when swollen with flood water. Walk across a broad moorland slope, keeping well to the left of the huge mountain ahead. Aim to avoid the steep, bouldery slopes and instead join the ridge to the left. There is a path running all the way up the ridge at a less severe gradient than a direct summit bid. The path climbs and crosses granite slabs at first, where it is necessary to look carefully for its continuation at times. Heather on the steep path later gives way to short grass, though the rounded ridge is scattered with boulders throughout the ascent. At the top there is a small tor of tilted granite blocks, then the path is more vague as it crosses the broad summit. There is a cairn at 716m marking the highest part of the mountain.

Walk across the short grass, passing low outcrops and boulders. Climb onto what appears to be a little tor, noting that there is a considerable gap on the far side. The steep and rocky slope bears a zig-zag path leading down to a gap. The path crosses granite slabs as it climbs uphill from the gap, and the narrow line can be traced past a couple of blocky tors to reach the summit of Beinn Bharrain at 721m. There is a cairn and a trig point, with extensive views in clear weather.

Look carefully for the path leaving the summit, picking a way roughly east and north-east down a rounded ridge of scoured,

A silhouette of Beinn Bharrain seen from low down on Machrie Moor

gritty soil and short grass. The slope becomes less steep, but also more bouldery and narrow. The lowest part of the ridge is Bealach an Fharaidh, where care should be taken to spot a path heading off to the right. Drop steeply downhill on a rather worn and stony path. Anyone wanting to avoid this route could walk on the rough, bouldery slopes to either side. When the slope begins to level out, masses of prostrate juniper can be seen amid the boulders and heather. Head directly across a rugged, boggy moorland slope, passing the outflow of little Dubh Loch on the way to the Allt Tigh an Shiorraim at the foot of Loch Tanna.

Head roughly south-west from the foot of Loch Tanna. The idea is to climb very gently across a rugged, boggy moorland to reach a broad gap between Beinn Bharrain and Sail Chalmadale. Cross this gap and descend into the head of Glen Scaftigill. The walking is fairly easy, though there is no trodden path at all. Cross grass, heather and bog myrtle on the gradual drift down towards the burn draining the glen. This is a bouldery, rocky burn and there are plenty of places where it can be crossed. After crossing, the ground on the far side is rather more rough and tussocky. Climb very gradually across the slopes of the glen, to reach the edge of a coniferous plantation seen straight ahead. The forest is bounded by a tall deer fence, and there is a sort of trodden path alongside it, probably trodden by deer.

Turn right to follow the deer fence over the top of a broad and boggy rise. As it starts to descend, there is a gateway on the left. Go through the gate and follow a ride into the forest for a short way. Turn right at a junction of rides and follow a vague path on the wide, grassy, heathery strip between the trees. At another junction of rides, turn right again, crossing a burn and joining a clear gravel track at the same time. Follow the track uphill on a broad, heathery ride. The track bends well to the right at the top of the rise at Roileag, and there are some views across Kilbrannan Sound to Kintyre.

The track descends very gradually across the forested slopes of Roileag and Ceann Reamhar, crossing one broad, heathery, unplanted swathe of moorland. When a junction of gravel tracks is reached, note that this point was passed earlier in the day. Turn left to continue downhill, passing both the tall gate at the edge of the forest and the next gate before the track zig-zags downhill past the mast. Simply continue downhill across the grass and bracken slope to end back on the road between Imachar and Whitefarland.

WALK 26
Pirnmill & Beinn Bharrain

Beinn Bharrain is the highest of the Pirnmill Hills grouped in the north-west of the Isle of Arran. It rises steeply above the straggly little village of Pirnmill. The village makes a handy starting point for

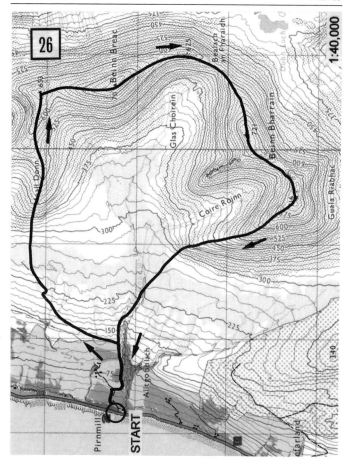

the walk and there is good access to a rugged moorland shelf. Paths are vague across the moorland shelf, though there is a fairly well trodden path along the mountain ridge high above. It is worth climbing Beinn Breac as well as Beinn Bharrain in order to make the most of the high ridge, although the ascent to the ridge by way of Meall Donn is steep and unremitting. In clear weather, views from

127

the ridge are remarkably extensive and take in all the highest peaks on the Isle of Arran.

The Route

Distance: 8 miles (13km)

Start: Anvil Tearoom, Pirnmill, grid ref 873443.

Terrain: Rugged hillwalking, mostly on good paths, but some areas have no paths.

Start at the Anvil Tearoom in Pirnmill. Face the tearoom, noting that there is a clear gravel track off to the left, running straight uphill from its junction with the main coastal road. The track swings to the left, passes a ruined tin-roofed building, then turns right and runs uphill. When the track bends to the left, don't follow it, but look carefully off to the right to spot a stile over a fence. A narrow and muddy path squeezes between densely planted young trees, but a more open stand of oak is encountered at a higher level. There are views between the oak trees over some fine, slender waterfalls deep within a gorge. Follow the path further uphill, crossing a couple of small stiles alongside a deer fence. Emerging into more open fields at a higher level, cross a ladder stile at the corner of the deer fence to reach an expanse of rugged moorland.

Start climbing uphill on the moorland slope, drifting to the left as height is gained. There are all sorts of vague paths across the uneven slopes of heather, grass and rock, including an overgrown path which exists only as a groove across the moor. If this feature is discovered, then follow it, otherwise simply make a bee-line towards Meall Donn, crossing a gentler slope of more boggy ground on the way. The steep slopes of Meall Donn are covered in heather and boulders, without any clear paths. Choose any route uphill, noting that the ground is less bouldery further to the left. The steep slope is unremitting, but taken steadily there is an eventual break of slope where the walking becomes easier. Follow the rounded, heathery, bouldery crest onwards and upwards. A path is eventually gained on another broad crest overlooking Fion Lochan. Turn right and follow this gently uphill to a broad and bouldery summit at 653m.

Continue straight along the rounded, bouldery crest, using a path which proves to be quite easy despite the boulders. The path

Looking along a bouldery ridge from Cir Mhor to Caisteal Abhail (Walk 24)
Beinn Bharrain rising across Glen Scaftigill from Sail Chalmadale (Walk 25)

Looking down on Catacol from the slopes of Meall nan Damh (Walk 28)
Lochranza Castle with Newton Point seen rising beyond (Walk 32)

leads to a large summit cairn on Beinn Breac at 711m. There is a sudden view straight ahead stretching beyond the Isle of Arran to the prominent pyramid of Ailsa Craig. Leave the summit and continue along the rounded, bouldery ridge, following a path which is rather vague in places. The ridge levels out on a shoulder, then there are larger boulders to be crossed on the way down to the gap of Bealach an Fharaidh. Climb uphill from the gap, stepping across some large boulders at first. The slope becomes less bouldery, but rather steeper too, featuring scoured gritty soil and short grass. The top of Beinn Bharrain is fairly broad, bearing a cairn and trig point at 721m.

Continue along the broad crest, walking on short grass, following a vague path and passing a couple of blocky little granite tors. The path remains narrow, but is more clearly trodden down to the next gap. Granite slabs are crossed just before the grassy base of the gap. A steep slope ahead bears a zig-zag path, which passes the rockier parts of a prominent granite tor. The top of this tor is a prominent summit in its own right, and this should be borne in mind in poor visibility. Drop down slightly from the tor and follow the path further across the broad summit, walking on short grass and passing low outcrops and boulders. There is a cairn at 716m marking the highest point on the mountain.

Continue across the broad summit, drifting to the right towards a small tor of tilted granite blocks. A path leaves the tor, running straight down a rounded ridge scattered with boulders. Later, the ground steepens a little and short grass gives way to heather. Look carefully for the line of the path after it runs onto granite slabs, then follow it down onto a gentler sloping, though more rugged moorland which can be boggy underfoot. Only a vague path crosses the lower moorland, so be sure to swing to the right to cross a river well before it plunges into a steep, wooded gorge. Stay well clear of the gorge on the final stage of the descent, aiming to reach the corner of the deer fence which was crossed earlier in the day's walk. Cross the ladder stile over the deer fence, then follow the narrow path downhill alongside the fence. Cross two smaller stiles as the path runs down through a woodland of birch and oak, looking into the gorge to spot some fine waterfalls. The path has a muddy stretch before a stile gives way to a firm track. Turn left and follow the track back down to Pirnmill.

Pirnmill

Penrioch was a farmstead of some antiquity from which the village of Pirnmill eventually grew. Apart from a history of smuggling, fishing was an important industry. The modern name of Pirnmill was derived from a mill which made bobbins, or "pirns", from around 1780 to 1840. The ruins of the old mill can still be seen. The little village has only a few features and facilities. Listed from south to north they include: toilets, war memorial, Anvil Tearoom, Pirnmill Primary School and the corrugated iron Church of Scotland. The beach is quite rough and bouldery.

WALK 27
Coire Fhion Lochain

There is a popular walk from Thundergay, up to Coire Fhion Lochain, which can be extended into a short horseshoe walk on the hills overlooking the water. Coire Fhion Lochain is sometimes rendered as Correin Lochain, which is probably a half-Anglicisation of the Gaelic pronunciation. While this walk is presented as a short hill walk, it can also double as an access route towards longer and tougher days on the hills. For instance, some walkers who put in all the effort necessary to climb Meall Biorach may prefer to stay high and continue over Beinn Breac and Beinn Bharrain.

The Route

Distance:	5¹/₂ miles (9km)
Start:	Mid Thundergay, grid ref 879466.
Terrain:	A straightforward hill walk mostly on good paths.

There is only a limited space in which to park alongside the main coastal road at Thundergay. The walk commences at the start of the access road serving a handful of houses at Mid Thundergay. There is a public footpath signpost reading "Correin Lochain", a small red postbox, and signs for Thundergay, Wellside and the Arran Pottery. Follow the stony access track which winds uphill to the Arran Pottery. A grassy surface continues past the last couple of houses.

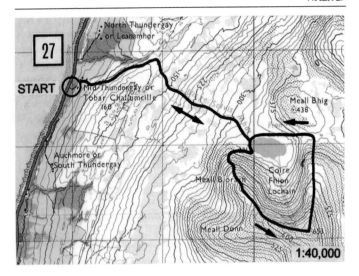

There are two gateways ahead and the one to pass through is the one on the right. There seems to be only a vague field path running uphill alongside a fence, but within a short while the course becomes much clearer, surfaced with stones or even crossing bare rock. Cross a ladder stile beside a gate in a tall deer fence.

The path runs across a heathery slope, with the dome of Meall nan Damh rising ahead. The path crosses a burn, then swings to the right to face Meall Biorach. An uphill pull runs alongside another burn which features a series of little waterfalls. Chase the burn upstream following the stony, bouldery path on a parallel course. A couple of sprawling cairns stand on the path a short way before the waters of Fion Lochan are reached. There is a fine gravelly beach formed of broken chips of granite. Other small beaches can be distinguished by looking across the loch. Some walkers are content to come this far and retrace their steps to Thundergay, but this walk is extended around Coire Fhion Lochain, embracing the hills overlooking the loch.

An anti-clockwise circuit ensures that paths are easily spotted, especially paths on the steep slopes of Meall Biorach. Start the circuit by turning right along the shore of Fion Lochan. Follow a

131

narrow, gritty path gently uphill and away from the shore. The path suddenly swings to the right and cuts across the steep, heathery lower slopes of Meall Biorach. As it climbs, the path becomes more bouldery. Watch carefully for a turning to the left, and continue zig-zagging uphill. The path takes a fairly easy course across the steep, rugged slope. At a higher level the gradient eases and there is a stretch along a level, rounded shoulder of low rocky outcrops, heather and gritty soil. The path crosses a large, gently sloping slab of granite, then rises in stages towards the main crest of the range. There is often a good view down onto Fion Lochan. A broad summit at 653m is covered in large boulders and short grass.

A number of vague paths converge on the bouldery summit, and by turning left the route can be continued around the head of Coire Fhion Lochain. There are more good views down over the loch from various points on the descent. A reasonably gentle, rounded ridge of outcropping slabs, gritty soil, sparse vegetation and scattered boulders is followed downhill. Later there is a steep slope of short heather leading down to a broad and boggy gap. Look out for a well trodden path cutting across the gap. Turn left to follow this path down from the gap, back towards Fion Lochan. The path descends a rugged slope to reach the waterside, then proceeds across the foot of a heathery slope to reach the burn flowing out of the loch. Cross over the burn and turn right to follow it downstream. The return route is simply a matter of retracing the earlier steps of the day, following the path back down to Mid Thundergay and the main coastal road.

Thundergay

The name Thundergay is also rendered as Thunderguy. It was one of a series of farmsteads dotted along the western side of the Isle of Arran, all of great antiquity. They included Thundergay, Penrioch, Altgobhlach, Imachar and Banleacainn. There are stories relating that the tenants held their tenancy from the Scottish kings. Some are said to have obtained their tenancy from a grateful Robert the Bruce in respect of services rendered during his long and bitter campaign to secure the Scottish throne, though there is no real evidence to support this.

WALK 28

Catacol & Meall Nan Damh

Meall nan Damh raises its rugged slopes almost directly south of Catacol. An ascent of the rocky dome can be combined with a descent alongside the lovely Fion Lochan. If the ascent commences at the small car park near Fairhaven, then the descent can rejoin the main coastal road at Thundergay. If a handy bus happens to be passing, then it can be used to return to Catacol, but in any case the coastal walk along the main road is pleasant, pursuing a roller-coaster route and clinging to a rugged slope overlooking Kilbrannan Sound.

The Route

Distance:	7¹/₂ miles (12km)
Start:	Fairhaven, near Catacol, grid ref 910489.
Terrain:	No paths on the rugged ascent, but paths, tracks and roads towards the end.

Fairhaven is a large white house offering accommodation a short way south of Catacol, where a bridge spans the river draining into Catacol Bay. There is a parking space beside the bridge, just on the south side close to Fairhaven. Start walking immediately from the back of the car park, following a clear, grassy, stony path parallel to the river. Go through a tall gate in a deer fence and cross a small campground where there is a large wooden hut. A narrower path continues onwards, crossing a squelchy area of heather and bog myrtle. There are a few trees on the hillside, and when the last of these have been passed, start climbing up the rugged slope. Heather and boulders have to be negotiated without the benefit of a trodden path. The minor summit of Meall nan Leac Sleamhuinn can be seen at the top of the slope, and this is a useful feature to head towards at first. Later, however, the loftier dome of Meall nan Damh is seen and a course should be steered towards the ridge on its right-hand side. A rugged moorland slope and a small stream need to be crossed before the ridge is gained.

A steep slope of uniform heather gives way to a slightly gentler slope of low rocky outcrops and scattered boulders. In clear weather a fine line of jagged peaks can be seen to the left, running from Caisteal Abhail to Beinn Nuis, while far away to the right, beyond Kintyre, are the Paps of Jura. The heather underfoot gets shorter and features little clubmosses, while the gradient gradually eases. The ground becomes more bouldery as a large cairn is passed, although the larger summit cairn is a bit further along and stands at 570m. There are fine views all around the Isle of Arran, but attention is

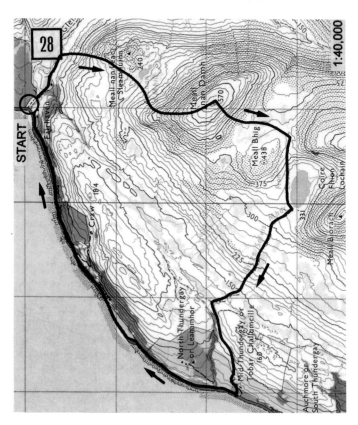

Meall nan Damh as seen from the summit of Beinn Tarsuinn

drawn to the gap beyond the moorland rise of Meall Bhig, where
this route is heading.

To leave the summit of Meall nan Damh, pick a way downhill
south-westwards and aim for a small pool on a broad moorland
gap. It is necessary to walk towards the edge of the hill before the
pool can be seen, then it is necessary to pick a careful way down the
steep slope to avoid extensive outcrops of rock. Pass the pool on its
left-hand side and forge straight across a moorland slope on the
eastern side of Meall Bhig. This tussocky bog features a narrow path
leading to another small pool on the next gap.

There is a clear path cutting across the gap, so turn right to
follow it into the huge hollow of Coire Fhion Lochain. The path
descends a rugged slope to reach the waterside and there are views
of three bright, gritty beaches around the shores of Fion Lochan. An
inspection of one of these beaches, after crossing the outflow from
the loch, reveals it to be made of broken chips of granite. Follow the
path downstream alongside the burn called Uisge Solvis Mhor. The
path passes a couple of sprawling cairns and pursues a stony,
bouldery course downhill. Note a series of fine waterfalls on the

descent, then watch for the path swinging to the right, crossing the burn as it flows downstream.

The path crosses a heathery slope and later there is a ladder stile beside a gate in a tall deer fence. The path crosses bare rock and stone, but at a lower level it becomes quite vague, although there is a fence which shows the way downhill. Go through a gate at the bottom of the field and turn left to continue down a grassy farm access track. A couple of houses and the Arran Pottery are passed in Mid Thundergay, while the track becomes stonier on the way down to the main coastal road.

Turn right to follow the coastal road. The first burn which is crossed is the Uisge Solvis Mhor, which was chased downstream from Coire Fhion Lochain. The next feature of note is an old burial ground. The road then clings precariously to a rugged slope, sometimes having cliffs above or below it, and featuring contorted sea stacks. There are plenty of trees clinging for survival on the upper cliffs, with heather and bracken on the lower slopes. Halfway back to Fairhaven the access track running up to Craw will be noticed off to the right. This was the last section of the coastal road encircling Arran to be completed. When Fairhaven is finally approached the road runs more sedately along a stretch of fairly level ground.

WALK 29

Catacol & Beinn Breac

Beinn Breac offers a fine, high-level walk along a smooth, whaleback ridge. The rugged dome of Meall nan Damh can be crossed as an enormous stepping stone on the way to Beann Breac and, after making a descent to lonely Loch Tanna, the two broad summits of Beinn Tarsuinn are included. There is a long descent into and through Glen Catacol to close the circuit. Beinn Breac is perched between the waters of Kilbrannan Sound and the highest peaks of Arran, so views in all directions prove most interesting in clear weather.

The Route

Distance: $10^{1}/_{2}$ miles (17km)

Start: Fairhaven, near Catacol, grid ref 910489.

Terrain: Rugged hill walking, often without trodden paths, so careful navigation is needed in mist.

Fairhaven is a large white house offering accommodation a short way south of Catacol, where a bridge spans the river draining into Catacol Bay. There is a parking space beside the bridge, just on the south side close to Fairhaven. Start walking immediately from the back of the car park, following a clear, grassy, stony path parallel to the river. Go through a tall gate in a deer fence and cross a small campground where there is a large wooden hut. A narrower path continues onwards, crossing a squelchy area of heather and bog myrtle. There are a few trees on the hillside, and when the last of these have been passed, start climbing up the rugged slope. Heather and boulders have to be negotiated without the benefit of a trodden path. The minor summit of Meall nan Leac Sleamhuinn can be seen at the top of the slope, and this is a useful feature to head towards at first. Later, however, the loftier dome of Meall nan Damh is seen and a course should be steered towards the ridge on its right-hand side. A rugged moorland slope and a small stream need to be crossed before the ridge is gained.

A steep slope of uniform heather gives way to a slightly gentler slope of low rocky outcrops and scattered boulders. In clear weather a fine line of jagged peaks can be seen to the left, running from Caisteal Abhail to Beinn Nuis, while far away to the right, beyond Kintyre, are the Paps of Jura. The heather underfoot gets shorter and features little clubmosses, while the gradient gradually eases. The ground becomes more bouldery as a large cairn is passed, although the larger summit cairn is a bit further along and stands at 570m. There are fine views all around the Isle of Arran, but attention is drawn to the smooth, whaleback ridge of Beinn Breac and lonely Loch Tanna, which are later to be visited on this route.

To leave the summit of Meall nan Damh, pick a way downhill south-westwards and aim for a small pool on a broad moorland gap. It is necessary to walk towards the edge of the hill before the pool can be seen, then it is necessary to pick a careful way down the

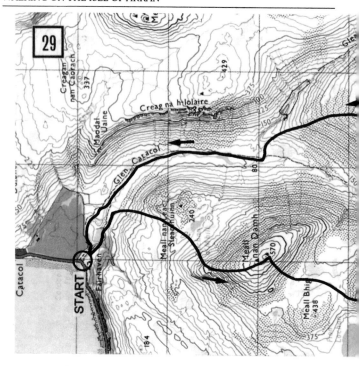

steep slope to avoid extensive outcrops of rock. Pass the pool on its left-hand side and forge straight across a moorland slope on the eastern side of Meall Bhig. This tussocky bog features a narrow path leading to another small pool on the next gap. Start climbing straight uphill, directly southwards from the gap, towards Beinn Breac. A short, steep slope of short heather gives way to a gentler slope of outcropping slabs, gritty soil, sparse vegetation and boulders. Follow this rounded shoulder further uphill, passing to one or the other side of a wrinkled outcrop at the top. There is a subsidiary summit at 653m where a number of vague paths converge, and there are fine views into Coire Fhion Lochain. Continue straight along the rounded, bouldery crest, using a path which proves to be quite easy despite the boulders. The path leads to a large summit

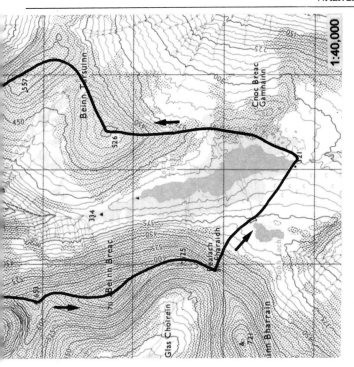

cairn at 711m. There is a sudden view straight ahead stretching beyond the Isle of Arran to the prominent pyramid of Ailsa Craig.

Leave the summit and continue along the rounded, bouldery ridge, following a path which is rather vague in places. The ridge levels out on a shoulder, then there are larger boulders to be crossed on the way down to the gap of Bealach an Fharaidh. Exit directly to the left from the gap, dropping steeply downhill on a rather worn and stony path. Anyone wanting to avoid this route could walk on the rough, bouldery slopes to either side. When the slope begins to level out, masses of prostrate juniper can be seen amid the boulders and heather. Head directly across a rugged, boggy moorland slope, passing the outflow of little Dubh Loch on the way to the Allt Tigh an Shiorraim at the foot of Loch Tanna.

Cross the Allt Tigh an Shiorraim where it flows from Loch Tanna, then turn left to start walking towards Beinn Tarsuinn. Following the shore of the loch is rather too rough and wet, so it is better to drift away from the shore and head northwards towards the hill. The moorland slope can be boggy and rocky in places, and as the ground steepens there is more prostrate juniper couched amid the rock and heather. The first part of Beinn Tarsuinn is broad, gritty, bouldery and features some low outcrops of granite. The only cairn is a small construction just off the 526m summit. Continue across the summit, down to a broad, boggy gap, then climb uphill towards a slightly higher part of Beinn Tarsuinn. Drift to the left on the ascent to reach the bouldery cairn on the bouldery summit at 557m. There is a fine view along a jagged line of peaks from Beinn Nuis to Caisteal Abhail, while in the opposite direction the Paps of Jura appear beyond Meall nan Damh.

Aim towards Meall nan Damh at the start of the descent, dropping down a steep slope of heather and boulders. Swing more towards the junction of Glen Catacol and Gleann Diomhan later, crossing a gentle, boggy slope before descending more steeply again. There is a vague path on the lower part of the descent. Swing to the left towards the end of the slope, aiming to pick up a clear path running through Glen Catacol. Turn right to follow the path, which generally runs close to the river, which in turn often runs across slabs of granite where only occasional boulders stand marooned. Small rapids and waterfalls can be enjoyed. The river has a more cobbly stretch and the ground alongside features a mixture of grass, heather, bracken and bog myrtle. When the river goes through a narrow constriction, the path climbs over an outcrop of banded rock. The final meanders of the river are faithfully traced and a ladder stile needs to be crossed before the main road is reached at a flat concrete bridge. Turn left to cross the bridge to return to the car park where the walk started.

Catacol

Catacol was no more than a poor clachan in the 1800s, but the land was acquired by the Hamiltons and things began to change. The illegitimate daughter of the eighth Duke, Ann Douglas, married Lord Rossmore from Ireland and received the lands around Catacol as a dowry. Lord Rossmore built a fine house where Catacol Farm now stands, as well as a church at Lenimore. There was no minister for the church at first, but when one was appointed a manse was built where the Catacol Hotel now stands. The terrace of houses known as the "Twelve Apostles" was built in the 1860s to house the people who were cleared from the older clachan. However, the people refused to live there and drifted elsewhere, and the terrace became known as "Hungry Row" until tenants were found. Facilities in the village are limited to the food, drink and accommodation provided by the Catacol Bay Hotel.

WALK 30
Catacol & Beinn Tarsuinn

Glen Catacol offers splendid access to the hills in the north-west of the Isle of Arran. While many walkers feel obliged to climb the highest hills, there are a handful of lesser heights which prove to be just as rugged, if not more so in places. The sprawling Beinn Tarsuinn can be climbed, followed by the steep and bouldery slopes of Beinn Bhreac. The broad moorland crest beyond is puncutated by the little hump of Beinn Bhiorach and the larger hump of Meall Mor. At the end of the walk, there is a splendid view along the length of Glen Catacol, not available from any other standpoint. The lack of paths across these hills suggests that most walkers are content to stay low in the glens, or on the higher mountains.

The Route

Distance:	10¹/₂ miles (17km)
Start:	Fairhaven, near Catacol, grid ref 910489.
Terrain:	Rugged hill walking, often without trodden paths.

Fairhaven is a large white house a short way south of the village of Catacol, where a bridge spans the river draining Glen Catacol. There is a parking space beside the bridge, just on the south side near Fairhaven. Start walking by crossing the bridge and turning right. A public footpath signpost offers destinations including

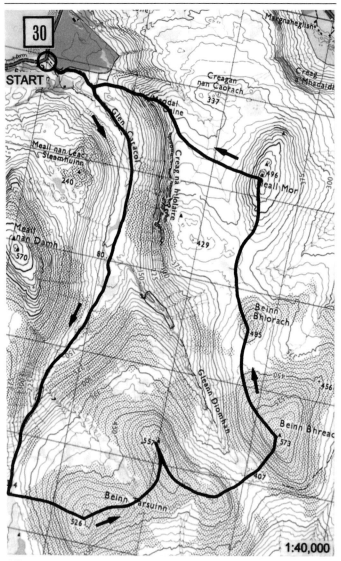

Gleann Diomhan and Loch Tanna. Follow a broad, grassy, stony path alongside the river and cross a ladder stile over a tall deer fence. The path continues to run alongside the river, then rises to cross an outcrop of banded rock. The river runs through a narrow constriction below the outcrop. The path runs alongside a cobbly stretch of the river, passing areas of grass, heather, bracken and bog myrtle.

Further upstream, the river runs across bare slabs of granite where occasional large boulders stand marooned. There are a couple of lesser paths branching off to the left leading up into Gleann Diomhan. A bouldery river needs to be forded and the path remains clear as it climbs towards the head of Glen Catacol. The surface is rather more bouldery and some sections can be boggy. The river often features small waterfalls and there are lengthy stretches where the water slides over a clean bed of granite. Off to the left is a steeper waterslide on the Allt nan Calman. Follow the river upstream as it diminishes, passing a sprawling cairn before reaching another cairn on a broad, stony gap. There is a view ahead of Loch Tanna.

Turn left to climb above the gap, ascending a steep slope of heather and boulders, before the gradient eases and there are fewer boulders. At length a small cairn is passed on an outcrop of granite slabs, though this is not quite on the 526m summit of Beinn Tarsuinn. The rest of the summit area is a broad expanse of low outcrops, boulders and gritty soil. Continue walking north-eastwards across the summit, drop down to a broad gap, then climb uphill towards a slightly higher summit of Beinn Tarsuinn. Drift to the left on the ascent to reach the cairn on the bouldery summit at 557m. There is a fine view along a jagged line of peaks from Beinn Nuis to Caisteal Abhail, while in the opposite direction the Paps of Jura appear beyond Meall nan Damh.

The next summit is Beinn Bhreac, but it should not be approached directly across Gleann Diomhan. Instead, walk south-eastwards along the crest of Beinn Tarsuinn, then gradually drift to the left until the direction is almost north-eastwards. There is a steep and bouldery descent from the crest of Beinn Tarsuinn to a broad gap of boggy ground and stony patches. Immediately ahead is the steep, intimidating and bouldery flank of Beinn Bhreac. The heather is quite deep and springy, interspersed with bilberry and crowberry, often concealing deep holes which need to be avoided. The bouldery parts of the slope need great care as some of the specimens are loose. On many parts it is necessary to use hands as well as feet to assist on the climb. The gradient eases near the top, with shorter heather, short grass and more deeply embedded boulders. There is a bouldery summit cairn standing at 573m.

Leave the top of Beinn Bhreac by walking north-west along a broad, rounded ridge, before swinging more northwards toward the rugged hump of Beinn Bhiorach. On the descent from Beinn Bhreac, a large, square cairn is passed, then after crossing a broad moorland gap a short climb leads up an easy, bouldery slope. The top of the little hill is a bare peak of rock at 485m. Continue walking over to the next broad gap, carefully picking a way down a short, steep slope which has some rocky areas. The next prominent hill in view is Meall Mor, and this is best approached by taking a direct line across an uneven slope of moorland. Climb straight up a blunt, rounded ridge, where scattered boulders on the heathery slope pose no problem. There is a cairn on the summit of Meall Mor at 496m, with another cairn further along the crest. There is a last chance to absorb the view before the descent.

Descend westwards from the summit, picking a careful way down a steep slope of heather, avoiding any areas of rock. Forge across an uneven tract of moorland, crossing a shallow valley and drifting to the right to reach the prow of Maodal Uaine. The rugged moorland underfoot gives way to a rounded spur of short heather descending more steeply into Glen Catacol. There is a splendid view along the length of the glen, which in its middle reaches is a perfect "U" shape. Descend more steeply, bearing to the right along a narrow path to avoid a rockstep to the left. The path descends through a notch in the rock, then continues down a brackeny slope, later passing close to a large boulder of granite. The gradient eases and by heading towards the river it is possible to join the path which was used at the start of the day's walk. Follow the path alongside the river, crossing the ladder stile over the tall deer fence, to return to the main road and car park across the bridge.

WALK 31
Lochranza & Meall Mor

Rising south of Lochranza is a rugged, rocky dome of a hill called Meall Mor. While a direct approach would be quite difficult, the hill can be climbed more easily by crossing it on the way from Glen Catacol to Gleann Easan Biorach. The main coastal road is followed from Lochranza to Catacol, although of course this could be covered by car or bus if desired. Fine views are available on the ascent, though much of the upland crossing is quite pathless and needs special care in mist. The descent and return to Lochranza is by way of the boggy Gleann Easan Biorach.

The Route
Distance: 6¹/₂ miles (11km)
Start: Lochranza Castle, grid ref 932507.
Terrain: Roads at first, then paths, giving way to rugged, pathless terrain.

The start of this walk could be anywhere in Lochranza, but Lochranza Castle makes a good reference point. Walk through the village in the direction of the Claonaig Ferry and continue along the road to leave Lochranza. The road runs round Coillemore Point and there is a track running parallel to the road just a short way inland. Follow the track, which passes a moss-bound heap of stones marked with the following words: "The Sailor's Grave. Here Lies John McLean. Died 12 August 1854." Follow the road past a solitary house. A rugged, vegetated, damp and wooded cliff rises above the road. There are a few small, damp caves and the cliff is a favourite nesting place for seabirds.

Passing through Catacol, note the Catacol Bay Hotel and the terrace of houses known as the Twelve Apostles. Leaving the village, there is a choice either of walking along the main road, or walking along the grassy and pebbly strip between the main road and the sea. Either way, a flat concrete bridge will be reached close to the large white house called Fairhaven. Don't cross the bridge, but turn left to leave the road and follow a path into Glen Catacol as indicated by a public footpath signpost. Follow a broad, grassy, stony path alongside the river and cross a ladder stile over a tall deer fence. The path continues to run alongside the river, then rises to cross an outcrop of banded rock. The river runs through a narrow constriction below the outcrop. The path runs alongside a cobbly stretch of the river, passing areas of grass, heather, bracken and bog

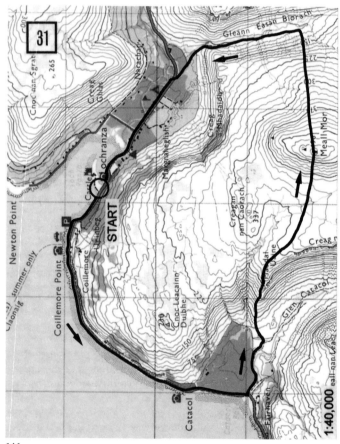

myrtle.

When the open floor of the glen is reached, drift leftwards away from the riverside path. Aim to walk through an area of bracken in the direction of the rocky prow of Maodal Uaine, passing a prominent large boulder on the way. A narrow path should be located, which leaves the brackeny slope and climbs up through a notch in the rock above. Keep strictly to the line of the path to negotiate the ascent of the rockstep. Once on top, note the splendid view along the length of Glen Catacol, which in its middle reaches is a perfect "U" shape. Continue climbing up a rounded spur of short heather, which gives way to more rugged moorland at a higher level. Leaving Maodal Uaine, it is necessary to forge straight across an uneven tract of moorland in the direction of Meall Mor. Looking ahead, pick any line of ascent towards the summit which seems to be free of rock. There are some strips of heather which allow steep, but relatively safe ascents. There is a cairn on the summit of Meall Mor at 496m, with another cairn further along the crest. Take a moment to absorb the view before the descent, which is remarkably extensive despite the modest elevation.

Walk roughly eastwards to descend from Meall Mor. The slope has outcrops of rock and boulders at first, though these begin to give way to more rugged, boggy moorland slopes. There are no paths on the way into Gleann Easan Biorach, and it is necessary to keep looking ahead to gauge the best line of descent. It is perhaps best to drift slightly to the left, in order to avoid being drawn into a watercourse which is mostly bare rock, but keep looking ahead in order to outflank any obstacles in good time. Eventually, a path will be reached which runs roughly parallel to the river draining the glen. Turn left to follow it downstream.

Enjoy a series of little waterfalls on the way down through Gleann Easan Biorach. The path is often braided across boggy ground and squelchy grassland, but inflowing burns offer the chance to get your boots cleaned from time to time. A firmer path is eventually joined where the river drops more steeply through a rocky gorge. Small waterfalls and rock pools are overlooked by the rocky dome of Torr Nead an Eoin. A stretch of safety fencing has been provided above a small water intake. The rocky path gives way to a broader track, which runs between a bridge and a cottage

Lochranza Castle catches a ray of sun on a dull day

to reach the main road.

Turn left to walk back through Lochranza, passing first the Isle of Arran Distillery, then later the campsite, Loch Ranza Field Studies Centre, Church of Scotland and Youth Hostel to return to Lochranza Castle, or whatever other place the walk commenced.

Lochranza Castle

There are two parts to Lochranza Castle. First there was a medieval hallhouse, with a heavily defended lower doorway and an upper doorway with a removable ladder. The owner may have been Sween, who married into the royal house of Connacht and was Lord of Knapdale in Argyll. When Robert the High Steward became King of Scotland in 1371, Lochranza became a royal castle. A later period of building incorporated Sween's castle into a rather more decorative structure. The building was completed by one of the Montgomery Earls of Eglinton, who had received estates on the Isle of Arran from James II in 1452. New doorways were created and old ones were blocked, and this remains apparent from a close study of the fabric. The Montgomeries lost their estates to the Hamiltons in 1705 and much later the castle fell ruinous. One whole corner collapsed during a storm in 1897, but the fabric has now been consolidated and has plenty of interesting features. The key can be obtained from the Post Office by anyone wishing to explore the interior.

War Grave

A monument near the Claonaig Ferry slipway has been erected to comemmorate the crew of a submarine which sank offshore during World War II. The inscription reads: "HMS/M Vandal sank $1^{1}/_2$ miles north west from here on 24th February 1943. She and her crew lie there still."

Isle of Arran Distillery

Completed only in 1997, the Isle of Arran Distillery buildings are quite modern, yet have a distinctly traditional shape. When it was being promoted, it was claimed to be the first legal distillery on the island for over 150 years. There are those who claim that when whisky was last distilled on the island it was the best in Scotland. Connoisseurs can now judge for themselves, testing the single malt against others in Scotland. The distillery caters for visitors.

WALK 32

Gleann Easan Biorach

There is a popular circuit into the hills of northern Arran from Lochranza to Catacol. The route doesn't climb any hills, but works its way through the glens and over a couple of bleak and boggy gaps. Starting from Lochranza, the route climbs up through Gleann Easan Biorach to reach Loch na Davie, then climbs over a gap on the slopes of Beinn Bhreac before descending through Gleann Diomhan and Glen Catacol. The main coastal road can be used to make a circular walk by leading from the village of Catacol back to Lochranza. The paths in Gleann Easan Biorach, Glen Catacol and Gleann Diomhan can be used to reach a variety of hills in the north-west of the Isle of Arran. Some of these walks are covered in other descriptions in this guide. This walk covers only the basic circuit from glen to glen.

The Route

Distance:	10 miles (16km)
Start:	Lochranza Castle, grid ref 932507.
Terrain:	Mostly rough, boggy, bouldery paths often running alongside rivers and burns.

The start of this walk could be anywhere in Lochranza, but Lochranza Castle makes a good reference point. Walk through the long and straggly village as if following the road over to Sannox, passing the Youth Hostel, Church of Scotland and Isle of Arran Distillery. Just beyond the distillery, and immediately before a humpback bridge, is a public footpath signpost on the right. The signpost points the way into Gleann Easan Biorach and a smaller sign announces that this is also the way to Loch na Davie. A clear track runs into the glen, but it quickly gives way to a steep, stony path climbing uphill. The path picks its way along the side of a rough and rocky slope, and a stretch of safety fencing has been provided above a small water intake point. A series of small waterfalls and rock pools are overlooked by the rocky dome of Torr Nead an Eoin. The path continues climbing and eventually runs more or less level across a broad and boggy moorland close to the river.

There are other small waterfalls to look at as the path runs further alongside the river. The path is often braided across boggy ground and squelchy grassland, but inflowing burns offer the chance to get your boots cleaned from time to time. The river often slides along a smooth bed of granite, and there is a tributary off to the left which has the same sort of appearance. The path then climbs uphill on a bouldery, heathery slope. In wet weather there may well be running water on the path. The climb leads up to a heathery gap where Loch na Davie's shallow waters can be seen to the left. Dozens of small boulders project from the water, while careful inspection of either end of the loch reveals that the water dribbles in opposite directions both into Gleann Easan Biorach and Glen Iorsa.

The path continues beyond Loch na Davie, passing a cairn and gradually swinging to the right and climbing up around the shoulders of Beinn Bhreac. A couple of smaller cairns help to keep walkers on course at times when the path becomes rather narrow and vague. There is a gradual climb to reach a broad, boggy and stony gap between Beinn Bhreac, to the right, and Beinn Tarsuinn, to the left. In mist, it is helpful to spot the start of the path leading down into the top end of Gleann Diomhan, just to be sure that the correct line is going to be followed later. There is a narrow, stony path running parallel to the burn on the eastern side. Anyone inadvertently walking along the western side would experience great difficulties later. On the way downhill, the path is braided in some boggy areas and is bouldery in others. There is a stepped series of small waterfalls, followed by a longer fall which is tucked out of sight of the path. A granite gorge leads through an area which has been surrounded by a tall deer fence. This is the Gleann Diomhan National Nature Reserve, and the fencing has been erected to keep deer and sheep from damaging or destroying rare Arran Service trees.

Continue along the rough path beside the deer fence. There is access to the fenced enclosure to facilitate walkers who wish to have a closer look at the trees, the rocky gorge, or the waterfalls deep inside the gorge. The path leaves the lower corner of the enclosure and begins to swing to the right as it leaves the glen. The ground

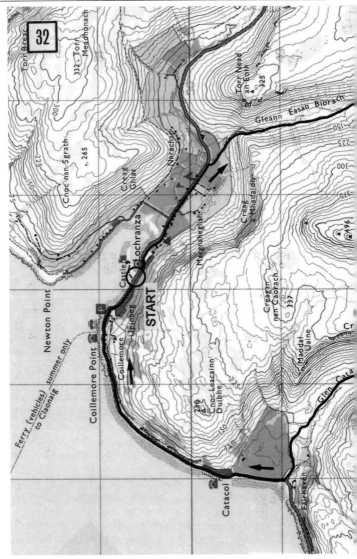

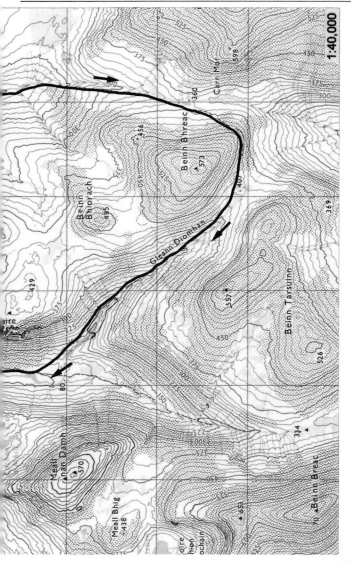

1:40,000

becomes firmer and drier, especially when areas of bracken are crossed. The path descends into Glen Catacol and joins a firm, clear path, which is followed by turning right. The path generally runs close to the river, which itself often runs across slabs of granite where only occasional boulders stand marooned. Small rapids and waterfalls can be enjoyed. The river has a more cobbly stretch and the ground alongside features a mixture of grass, heather, bracken and bog myrtle.

The river goes through a narrow constriction, while the path climbs over an outcrop of banded rock. The final meanders of the river are faithfully traced and a ladder stile needs to be crossed before the main road is reached at a flat concrete bridge. There is a public footpath signpost pointing back into the glen, a car park just across the bridge, and a pebbly raised beach across the road hidden behind gorse bushes. Turn right to follow the main road towards the village of Catacol, or alternatively walk on the grass or pebbles along the shore. The cottages known as the Twelve Apostles are passed, as well as the Catacol Bay Hotel. Some walkers might like to arrange to be collected at Catacol, or wait for a bus to Lochranza, but others will realise that the walk between the two villages is quite short and easy.

Some houses look across the road to a rocky shore, while later the shore is more bouldery. Inland, a rugged, vegetated, damp and wooded cliff rises above the road. There are a few small, damp caves and the cliff is a favourite nesting place for seabirds. Pass a solitary house, then later take a short track to the right of the road, staying at the foot of the wooded cliff. A moss-bound heap of stones is marked with the following words: "The Sailor's Grave. Here Lies John McLean. Died 12 August 1854." Continue following the road round Coillemore Point, passing toilets, car parking spaces and the Claonaig Ferry. The road continues through the village of Lochranza, returning walkers to Lochranza Castle.

Lochranza

The long and straggly village of Lochranza sits beside a sea loch and for a long time the only real access was from the sea. It was named Ranza by Norse settlers, while Scott penned poetry about it in *Lord of the Isles*. There is a fine range of features and facilities. Working through the village southwards from the Claonaig Ferry slipway these include: toilets, Lochranza Tearoom, butcher, guest houses, Lochranza Hotel and car park, Lochranza Castle, Castlekirk B&B, Castle Crafts, Post Office Store, Lochranza Village Hall, tennis court, Lochranza Youth Hostel, Church of Scotland, surgery, Loch Ranza Field Studies Centre, Apple Lodge Guest House, Lochranza Golf Club, Caravan and Camp Site, and finally the Arran Distillery. Walkers who complete the full circuit described above will pass everything!

Gleann Diomhan National Nature Reserve
The securely fenced enclosure high in Gleann Diomhan seems incongruous in its wilderness setting, but it is necessary to prevent sheep and deer from damaging two rare species of tree which thrive there. *Sorbus Arranensis* and *Sorbus pseudo-fennicus* both have a roothold in the glen. They are Whitebeam, or Service Trees, of the same genus as the Rowan, and bearing clusters of berries when in fruit. They grow apparently from bare rock, needing very little soil to secure a root-hold. These two species are unique to the Isle of Arran and are therefore given the protection of a secure fence. There is a ladder stile allowing access to walkers who wish to explore further.

WALK 33
Lochranza & Cock of Arran

The walk around the Cock of Arran from Lochranza is one of the classic coastal walks on the Isle of Arran. Lochranza is a long and straggly village which sits beside a charming sea loch. The romantic Lochranza Castle overlooks the waters from a narrow, grassy, pebbly point. The walk around the coast could be structured to link Lochranza with the distant village of Sannox, but this particular route description heads only for the remote Laggan Cottage, then crosses back over the hills to return to Lochranza. The rest of the coastal walk is covered in another route based on Sannox (Walk 35).

The Route

Distance:	8 miles (13km)
Start:	St. Bride's Church, Lochranza, grid ref 937503.
Terrain:	Roads, tracks and rugged coastal paths. Some parts can be muddy and rocky.

The walk could be started anywhere in the straggly village of Lochranza, but for the purpose of defining a place, start near St. Bride's Church of Scotland or the Loch Ranza Field Studies Centre. There is a signpost beside the road at this point indicating such varied destinations as the Fairy Dell, Ossian's Cave, the Cock of Arran and Laggan. Follow the minor road past the Lochranza Surgery, crossing a bridge and continuing past a golf course. At a junction with another minor road there are two public footpath signposts. Turn left to follow the road past some cottages to reach a pebbly beach at the head of Loch Ranza. Almost immediately on reaching the beach, turn right along a stony track. This quickly turns left and proceeds uphill between lines of trees. The track reaches a cottage called The Whins, which is the "Home of the Arran Stonemen". Crafts of all kinds, but most especially decorated stones, are available for purchase.

The track continues across a rugged slope of bracken and gorse scrub. Keep left to follow a track downhill towards a cottage called The Knowe. Ford a small burn below the cottage and continue along a squelchy moorland path. The path runs down to a cottage and wooden hut beside the sea at the foot of the wooded Fairy Dell. Turn right to walk along a coastal path, where short green grass offers an easy surface between bracken and the rugged shore. Later, a huge boulder is passed and there is little difference between walking on the beach or on the slope above it, as both are littered with large boulders of coarse conglomerate rock. This area is known as the Scriodan. Either follow the most well trodden line between the boulders, or if the tide is low, then there might be an easier way along the beach.

After wrestling with the boulders, there is an easier stretch of path and another large boulder features an overhanging projection which is sometimes good enough to offer protection from the rain. The coastal path continues easily along another ribbon of short
156

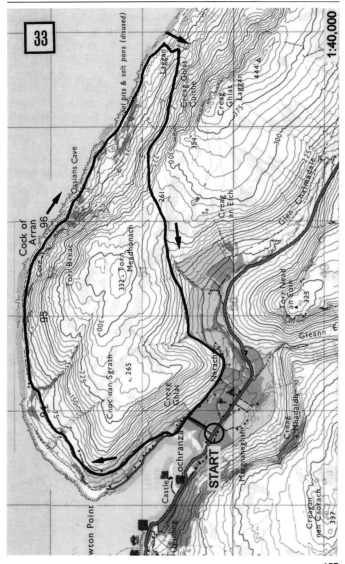

1:40,000

Wood pits & salt pans (disused)

Laggan

Creag Ghlas
Cuithe

Creag
Ghlas Laggan

444 △

375

354

300

Glen Chalmadale

261

Creag
an Eich

225

Ossians Cave

Cock of Arran

96

95

Torr Breac

334 · Torr
Meadhonach

Torr Nead
an Eoin

325

Gleann E

300

265

Creag
Ghlè

Narachan

Creag
a Mhadaidh

Castle

Lochranza

Creagan
nam Caorach

337

Maoineaglean

START

Newton Point

Ullinbeg

157

green grass, and the ruins of a couple of stone huts might be noticed in the bracken alongside. There is one level stretch which has been used as a field in the past, and curiously there is a natural igneous dyke forming a boundary wall between the field and the beach. The path crosses a drystone wall belonging to Cock Farm, whose ruins are out of sight further uphill. Also out of sight uphill is Ossian's Cave. Keep to the path closest to the rocky shore, taking care over ankle-wrenching terrain. There are boulders and muddy patches to negotiate.

The ruins of some buildings beside the sea once housed a little industrial site where coal was mined and saltpans were in use. The path crosses another rocky area, but gets a little easier later. Look out for a roughed-out circular millstone complete with a central hole just to the left of the path. The white form of Laggan Cottage appears quite suddenly after crossing a low outcrop of rock. Leave the isolated cottage by walking straight uphill, passing alongside the former kitchen garden.

The path is a clear, grassy ribbon which zig-zags uphill between areas of bracken. There are some drystone walled enclosures off to the left, then the path swings to the right and cuts across a steep and roughly vegetated slope. Looking downhill the ruins of Cock Farm and its associated drystone walls can be seen. As the path climbs it is flanked by heather and its surface becomes quite stony. At the top of the path there is a broad moorland gap to be crossed, where a cairn and small boulder stand beside the path.

The path is boggy and braided on the first part of the downhill run. Later, it becomes one clear line again, often running in a slight rut, surfaced with stones in some parts and crossing bare rock in other parts. There is generally a view over the Arran Distillery all the way downhill. The only time this passes from view is when the path nips into a wooded ravine to cross a small burn using a footbridge. The path runs down onto a clear, broad track and turns right. The track continues gently downhill, eventually passing the entrance to Butt Lodge Hotel, which was once used by shooting parties. The entrance of the Lochranza Studio Gallery is also passed. Turn left along the minor road used at the start of the walk, crossing the golf course and bridge to return to the main road near the church and field studies centre.

The Claonaig Ferry with Newton Point seen rising beyond

Cock Farm

The tumbled remains of Cock Farm are a sad reminder of how well populated the Isle of Arran once was. There were once over a hundred people living in the area now enclosed by Laggan and Cock Farm, yet not a single person lives there now. Cock Farm's greatest claim to fame concerns the Macmillan family. Malcolm Macmillan was born there in 1735 and he was the grandfather of Daniel Macmillan who founded the famous Macmillan publishing house. Malcolm was also the great-great grandfather of the Prime Minister Harold Macmillan. Cock Farm was finally deserted in 1912 and now lies mouldering in a brackeny hollow.

WALK 34

Lochranza & Sail an Im

Few walkers would consider climbing Sail an Im without continuing along the fine mountain ridge to the summit of Caisteal Abhail.

Even fewer walkers would consider climbing Sail an Im from Lochranza. In fact, there is an entertaining circuit available which uses traces of an old road over the Boguillie, linking Glen Chalmadale with North Glen Sannox. Sail an Im can then be climbed from the glen, with a return to Lochranza made directly along the broad moorland crest terminating at Torr Nead an Eoin. There is a surprise view of the village and the sea loch before the final descent.

The Route

Distance:	10¹/₂ miles (17km)
Start:	Arran Distillery, Lochranza, grid ref 493497.
Terrain:	Good paths at first, then pathless moorland slopes.

Start near the Isle of Arran Distillery set well back from the sea at Lochranza. Follow the main road uphill from a humpback bridge, passing the farm of Bellarie while skirting round the lower slopes of Torr Nead an Eoin. Turn left and follow a farm access track downhill, either fording the river in Glen Chalmadale, or crossing an adjacent footbridge. Turn right to follow the river upstream, walking along a track, passing a building and continuing along a path. The aim is to pick up the course of an old road running up through the glen, but the course is unclear at first. Follow the river upstream, until forced uphill to pass a pronounced bend where there is a short, steep, wooded slope. A clearer path continues immediately beyond.

The old highway shows some traces of engineering, but is little trodden these days and some parts are quite vague. The old way rises roughly parallel to the current main road, but on the opposite side of the river. The path rises gently across a slope of grass, bracken and heather. A handful of stunted trees are passed, then three small watercourses are crossed as the path continues to rise. A fourth stream is more powerful and could result in wet feet after wet weather. The burn is filled with trees and fine waterfalls. The path continues a little more steeply uphill, now climbing above the level of the main road over the Boguillie, but the gradient quickly eases on the higher moorlands. The path can be vague in places as it crosses areas of grass and heather, but with care it should be possible to distinguish its course at all times.

The path is little more than a groove contouring across the

Overlooking Lochranza from a perch on Torr Nead an Eoin (Walk 34)
Taking a break and enjoying Glen Sannox below Suidhe Fhearghas (Walk 36)

The rugged face of Beinn Nuis rises proudly above the glen (Walk 40)
Flat slabs of granite are reached on top of Goat Fell (Walk 41)

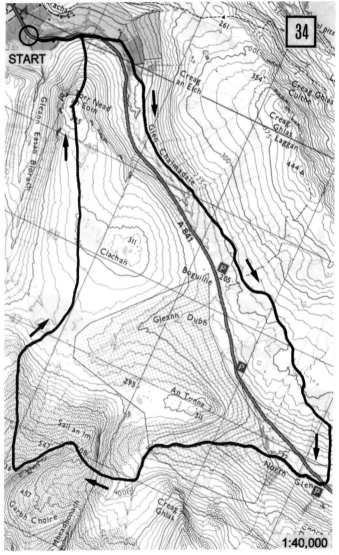

34

START

1:40,000

moorland. It climbs a little to cross a runnel of water, then drops downhill to pass the lower corner of an enclosure. The enclosure contains a handful of stunted trees and the tall fence protects them from damage by grazing deer. The groove is little more than a boggy trough in places, but it is sometimes flanked by boulders and can be quite clear. A couple of little burns are crossed by their original stone slab bridges, and an outcrop of bedrock has a splash of white quartz. The old track turns downhill as a clear ribbon of boggy grass across a rugged moorland slope. The track may carry running water for a while, then there is a paved ford through a small burn. The route contours for a while across a steeper slope, then there is a gate and stile in a tall deer fence. There is a rocky ford through a small burn where there are a few trees. The path continues as a short-cropped grassy ribbon flanked by bracken. The downhill run twists and turns, but in the main heads straight towards North Sannox. There is another ford across a wooded burn, then the path continues downhill and reaches a final ford and fence. Walk down towards the river and turn right to reach a road bridge.

Cross the bridge to reach a small car park, then turn immediately right and follow a riverside path. Note the fine waterfall pouring beneath the bridge, before picking a way along the squelchy, muddy path flanked by grass, heather and bog myrtle. A couple of small burns need to be forded, then a ladder stile is crossed beside a gate in a deer fence. The path runs between a stand of forestry and the river, passing many fine waterfalls as it climbs. The path is narrower at a higher level and features deeper heather. There is another stile leaving the top side of the forest and the path continues upstream, with fine views of Caisteal Abhail and the rocky cleft of Ceum na Caillich - the Witch's Step.

Leave the path by fording the river at some convenient point, then continue uphill, drifting gradually away from the river. The rugged face of Sail an Im is ahead, and by keeping to its left-hand side a relatively easy ascent can be made. A steep slope of heather and boulders also features low outcrops of granite which are pitched at an angle easy enough to be walked up without difficulty. A rounded, heathery summit has a scattering of boulders at 508m. There is a sudden view over to Lochranza. Turn left to pick up a narrow path which runs roughly south-west along the rounded ridge. The climb is on grass and heather, with some boulders and ribs of granite. Climb until a rounded granite hump is reached on top of a buttress overlooking the Garbh Choire, at 636m. While it is possible to continue along the ridge to the summit of Caisteal Abhail, this route now changes course and proceeds directly back to Lochranza.

Head downhill, roughly northwards to the distant hump of Torr Nead an Eoin. In clear weather it is worth surveying the terrain from a good height before negotiating it. Start the descent by dropping down a slope of grass, heather and boulders. The terrain is actually fairly easy at first, but later there is a swing to the right and a steeper fall towards a broad, boggy gap. A number of paths can be seen cutting across the bleak moorland slope, and any of them might be used. Crossing the broad gap is usually wet underfoot and there are a handful of small burns to be crossed. There is a slight ascent on an uneven heathery moorland at Clachan. There are small pools to be avoided and in clear weather the hump of Torr Nead an Eoin can be seen at the end of the broad crest.

When Torr Nead an Eoin is finally climbed, the short ascent reveals a couple of small cairns overlooking Lochranza. It is worth walking a little further in the direction of Lochranza to enjoy a splendid bird's-eye view of the village, but note that it is not possible to make a direct descent as there is steep rock tucked out of sight. More distant views encompass much of northern Arran, as well as looking across to the Paps of Jura beyond Kintyre. The final descent should be made in the direction of a solitary white farmhouse seen across the main road well to the right. The steep slope features short vegetation, although there is bracken at a lower level. A narrow path can be joined running alongside a fence, leading straight down to the main road. Turn left down the road, passing the Isle of Arran Distillery on the way back into Lochranza.

Isle of Arran Distillery
See Walk 31.

The Boguillie
The "new" road over the Boguillie was constructed between Lochranza and Sannox in 1843. Up to that point, most traffic

reaching Lochranza came from the sea, as the tracks eastwards over the Boguillie or southwards along the Craw were simply too rough and narrow to travel easily. Even when the "new" road was built, there were fords rather than bridges, and it was only barely possible for two carts to pass each other.

WALK 35

Sannox & Creag Ghlas Laggan

The coastal walk around the northern part of Arran is a popular excursion. It is possible to walk all the way from Sannox to Lochranza along rugged coastal paths, but the route described below is a circular tour, taking in the Fallen Rocks, Millstone Point, Laggan Cottage and summit of Creag Ghlas Laggan. The course of an old highway can be traced back towards Sannox, running parallel to the

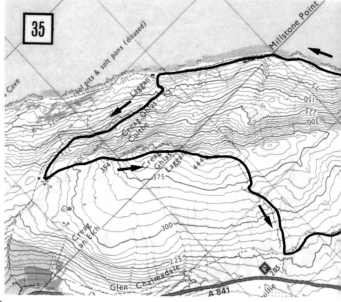

main road over the Boguillie. The route could be extended either along the coast to Lochranza, or after climbing up from Laggan Cottage a descent could be made along a clear path and track to Lochranza.

The Route

Distance:	10 miles (16km)
Start:	North Sannox Picnic Area, grid ref 015466.
Terrain:	Coastal tracks and paths, followed by moorlands with some clear paths and tracks.

Start at the North Sannox Picnic Area, signposted off the main road just above Sannox on the way to Lochranza. The car park is at the end of a short minor road, beside the sea. Anyone arriving by bus will easily be able to cover the distance to the sea from the main road. There are picnic tables and toilets available. A track continues from

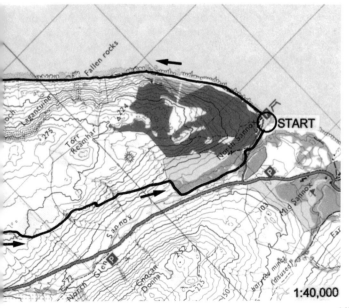

the end of the tarmac road and enters a forest using a tall gate in a deer fence. Follow the track along what is actually a raised beach covered in vegetation. A mixture of deciduous trees screen views of the more regimented forest beyond. A rugged rockface in the trees was once the coastline and has some small caves and undercut parts. Pass a prominent coastal marker pole and follow a line of telegraph poles to the edge of the forest.

Cross a ladder stile beside a gate in a tall deer fence, then follow the path onwards to cross an outcrop of conglomerate rock. The path continues easily through the Fallen Rocks; a chaotic jumble of massive conglomerate boulders strewn between a high cliff and the sea. Follow the path beyond the boulders, still tracing the line of telegraph poles onwards. The poles eventually run uphill towards another coastal marker post, high in a corrie where the ruined farmstead of Lagantuine is located. Stay low on the coastal path, which is grassy in most places, but pebbly, wet or muddy in other places. There are a series of small caves just above the path on the way to Millstone Point. The first cave is quite roomy and shows obvious signs of having been used for overnight accommodation. The others are smaller and unsuitable for human occupancy. Millstone Point is eventually turned and the little white Laggan Cottage will be seen ahead. The path remains easy all the way to the cottage.

Leave the isolated cottage by walking straight uphill, passing alongside the former kitchen garden. The path is a clear, grassy ribbon which zig-zags uphill between areas of bracken. There are some drystone walled enclosures off to the left, then the path swings to the right and cuts across a steep and roughly vegetated slope. Looking downhill the ruins of Cock Farm and its associated walls can be seen. As the path climbs it is flanked by heather and its surface becomes quite stony. At the top of the path there is a broad moorland gap to be crossed, where a cairn and small boulder stand beside the path.

Turn left to leave the clear path and start walking along a heather and grass moorland crest. By walking close to the edge overlooking the sea, it is possible to use a series of vague sheep paths, but it is just as easy to stay on the crest and aim more directly for the top of Creag Ghlas Laggan. There is a rounded rise before the

Lonely Laggan Cottage stands above a bouldery beach

main summit is reached. The main summit bears a trig point at 444m. Continue along the moorland crest to start the descent, but head off to the right before reaching a gap followed by another broad rise. Pick a way down the rugged moorland slope, crossing areas of heather and grass which may be boggy in places. A scant path marked on the map is practically absent on the ground, although it is more clearly defined closer to the road at the Boguillie.

While it is indeed possible to walk straight down to the road at the Boguillie and head straight back towards Sannox, there is also another route which could be sampled. There are traces of a former highway running parallel to the main road, but at a higher level on the hillside. The course of the old track is not too clear on the descent

167

from Creag Ghlas Laggan, but if a groove is spotted to the left, near a boulder, then this is the line to follow.

The groove contours across the moorland, climbs a little to cross a runnel of water, then drops downhill to pass the lower corner of an enclosure. The enclosure contains a handful of stunted trees and the tall fence protects them from damage by grazing deer. The groove is little more than a boggy trough in places, but it is sometimes flanked by boulders and can be quite clear. A couple of little burns are crossed by their original stone slab bridges, and an outcrop of bedrock has a splash of white quartz. The old track turns downhill as a clear ribbon of boggy grass across a rugged moorland slope. The track may carry running water for a while, then there is a paved ford through a small burn. The route contours for a while across a steeper slope, then there is a gate and stile in a tall deer fence. There is a rocky ford through a small burn where there are a few trees. The path continues as a short-cropped grassy ribbon flanked by bracken. The downhill run twists and turns, but in the main heads straight towards North Sannox. There is another ford across a wooded burn, then the path continues downhill and reaches a final ford and fence. There is no gate in the fence, but there is a gate and stile a short way downhill.

Alternatively, there is a riverside path, although in its lower, wooded reaches the path is very muddy and it is better to climb up to the farm access road before reaching the road bridge. Pony trekking is offered at North Sannox and there are always a variety of horses, ponies and even donkeys grazing in the fields. Follow the farm access road to a minor road. Either turn left to return to the North Sannox Picnic Area and car park, or turn right to reach the main road and bus service. The nearest places offering food and drink are in the village of Sannox. Head either for the Corrie Golf Club Tearoom or the Ingledene Hotel.

Sannox

The Sannox area is one of the places on the Isle of Arran with abundant ancient remains, dating from the Neolithic and Bronze Age. The name Sannox is believed to have Viking origins and the area remained well settled with numerous clachans and shielings. A Congregational Church was built in 1822, but the area was cleared of much of its population a few years later. It is known that many of them settled in Megantic County in Canada. The only real industry was a small barytes mine, which was opened in Glen Sannox in 1840. In 1862 the eleventh Duke of Hamilton closed it as it was becoming an eyesore, but it reopened during the Great War and finally closed when it was exhausted in 1938. It had its own little railway running to a pier, but these were removed, leaving only the ruins of a few buildings. Sannox has a small range of features and facilities which, listed from south to north, include: Gowanlea Guest House, Cliffdene Guest House, Ingledene Hotel, car park and toilets, Sannox Christian Centre, Sannox Congregational Church, Corrie Golf Club and Tearoom, and Sannox House B&B.

WALK 36

North Glen Sannox Horseshoe

There is a fine horseshoe walk around North Glen Sannox, though the initial part of the walk crosses boggy, forested ground on the floor of the glen. After a rugged climb onto Sail an Im, the route climbs high around the "Dress Circle" ridge to reach the summit of Caisteal Abhail. This much is fairly straightforward, but the continuation involves crossing the notorious cleft of Ceum na Caillich, or the Witch's Step, calling for a good head for heights and scrambling skills. In poor weather routes involving the Witch's Step are best avoided, and in really bad weather walkers would be well advised to descend either the way they came, or into the head of Glen Sannox for a boggy walk-out in relative safety.

The Route

Distance:	6¹/₂ miles (11km)
Start:	North Glen Sannox Bridge, grid ref 993467.
Terrain:	Boggy and rocky at first, then later involving some exposed and arduous scrambling.

There is a car park beside a bridge in North Glen Sannox, where a path runs alongside the river. Note the fine waterfall pouring

169

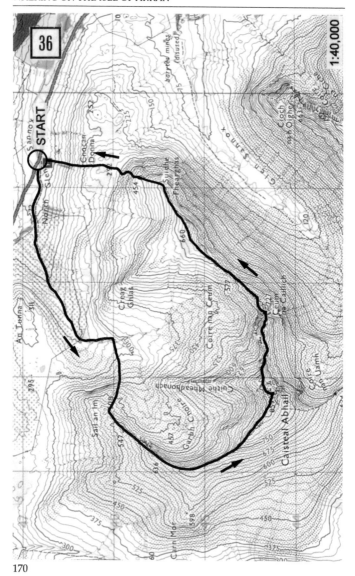

beneath the bridge, before picking a way along the squelchy, muddy path flanked by grass, heather and bog myrtle. A couple of small burns need to be forded, then a ladder stile is crossed beside a gate in a deer fence. The path runs between a stand of forestry and the river, passing many fine waterfalls as it climbs. The path is narrower at a higher level and features deeper heather. There is another stile leaving the top side of the forest and the path continues upstream, with fine views of Caisteal Abhail and the rocky cleft of Ceum na Caillich, or the Witch's Step.

Leave the path by fording the river at some convenient point, then continue uphill, drifting gradually away from the river. The rugged face of Sail an Im is ahead, and by keeping to its left-hand side a relatively easy ascent can be made. A steep slope of heather and boulders also features low outcrops of granite which are pitched at an angle easy enough to be walked up without difficulty. A rounded, heathery summit has a scattering of boulders at 508m. There is a sudden view over to Lochranza. Turn left to pick up a narrow path which runs roughly south-west along the rounded ridge. The climb is on grass and heather, with some boulders and ribs of granite. Climb until a rounded granite hump is reached on top of a buttress overlooking the Garbh Choire, at 636m.

Continue climbing at a fairly gentle gradient along the ridge, which gradually bends to the left as it approaches Caisteal Abhail. Some walkers call this ridge the Dress Circle, and it offers splendid views in clear weather. The top of Caisteal Abhail features a handful of blocky granite tors which have the appearance of ruined castles. On a fine day they offer a host of interesting scrambling routes. The main summit is on one of these tors, ending with a granite slab at 859m, which is easily gained. Views take in all the intricate details of Cir Mhor and the ridges leading to Goat Fell and Cioch na h' Oighe. Further afield the rest of Arran is well displayed in its setting in the Clyde. Several portions of the mainland, Kintyre, Jura and Antrim can be seen.

Leave the summit of Caisteal Abhail by tracing a ridge path roughly eastwards. The path passes a couple of blocky tors, which adventurous walkers might like to scramble across. The path runs out onto a deceptively gentle, grassy shoulder, then drops down more ruggedly to a bouldery gap. Rising above this gap is a rocky,

The summit slab of Caisteal Abhail provides an airy perch

blocky sawtooth ridge, which is best avoided by tracing a path across the Glen Sannox flank of the ridge. Just before reaching the Witch's Step, there is another bouldery tor furnishing a short scramble.

Crossing the Witch's Step calls for care and attention, a good head for heights and a willingness to use hands as well as feet. The descent into the gap is on granite slabs which fall quite steeply. Always look for signs of previous passage, and use the available hand and foot holds. Don't drop down to any place without being confident that the move can be reversed. While the broad slabs can be unnerving, there are useful steps encountered on the final few steps down into the gap. The gap is a worn, yet sharp ridge.

Towering above it is a steep and blocky granite peak which walkers will be pleased to hear that they don't need to climb. Exit to the left of the gap, picking a way down a rather worn gully. Look to the right for a short scramble uphill, which shows obvious signs of use. A narrow path picks its way round a steep and rocky slope. There is another short scramble up some jammed boulders, then the path works its way back towards the main ridge. A moment's pause is in order at this point.

The ridge is fairly narrow as it descends, but there is a good path which cuts through the heather and crosses ribs of granite. A large boulder is passed before the next gap is reached. The path then climbs up a broader ridge featuring short grass, heather, low outcrops and boulders of granite. There is a minor summit to cross, followed by a little gap, then a worn and gritty path runs uphill onto Suidhe Fhearghas. This point is mostly rock with a little short grass and heather. There is a pointed block projecting over Glen Sannox which makes the summit more easily identified in mist. The altitude is 660m and views take in the whole of Glen Sannox, with Beinn a' Chliabhain filling the deep gap of The Saddle.

The path runs plainly down the ridge in a series of giant steps separated by short level stretches. There are low outcrops and boulders amid the grass and heather, while areas of rotting granite make the path rather gritty. Towards the end of the ridge there is a spread of gritty ground followed by a broad, low outcrop of granite. Beyond that point there is a sudden steepening towards Sannox. The path swings to the left and runs steep and stony down a rugged slope. Note that there is a slab of rock to be crossed towards the foot of the slope. This can be avoided by taking action well in advance. Look out for a rowan tree in a gully and cut off to the left well above it, following a vague path which introduces a loop into the descent. This loop later swings right and runs beneath the slab.

There is a broad, boggy, heathery gap at the foot of this slope, where paths can be distinguished heading to left and right. The path heading left is rather vague, and it crosses the gap and keeps to the left of a couple of hummocky, heathery hills. Looking over the edge in clear weather, the car park in North Glen Sannox can be seen beside the bridge. Closer to hand, and still below, the very tops of some trees can be seen. Keep to the right of these trees and walk down the heathery slope alongside. Heather gives way to bracken on the steep slope and a vague path runs straight down to the car park. A little squelchy ground is crossed before the car park and main road are reached.

WALK 37

Glen Sannox Horseshoe

The Glen Sannox Horseshoe offers a day of high adventure and the circuit is one of Arran's mountain classics. Note at the outset that the route involves several rocky scrambles. The four most serious are the ascent of Cioch na h'Oighe, the descent from North Goat Fell, the ascent of Cir Mhor and the traverse of Ceum na Caillich - The Witch's Step. Time will be lost at each of these points, especially when travelling as part of a group. The escape from The Saddle into Glen Sannox is itself a scramble down the steep and rocky Whin Dyke. In foul weather, the Glen Sannox Horseshoe should not be attempted, but in clear, dry weather competent, tough scramblers will find it a most entertaining round.

The Route

Distance:	10 miles (16km)
Start:	Glen Cottage, Sannox, grid ref 016454.
Terrain:	Rough mountain walking, with some clear paths on rocky ground. Serious rock scrambling is required in places.

Start in between Sannox and Sannox Bridge, where there is roadside parking available near a riverside toilet block. Directly opposite the car park is Glen Cottage and a sign indicates the start of the cart track into Glen Sannox. Go through a tall gate and follow the narrow tarmac track uphill. It seems to head directly for Cioch na h'Oighe, but quickly bends to the right at a series of small graveyards. The track is rough and cobbly as it continues uphill and there is another tall gate to pass through. Tall white coastal marker posts stand either side of the track, then there is a fine view around Glen Sannox
174

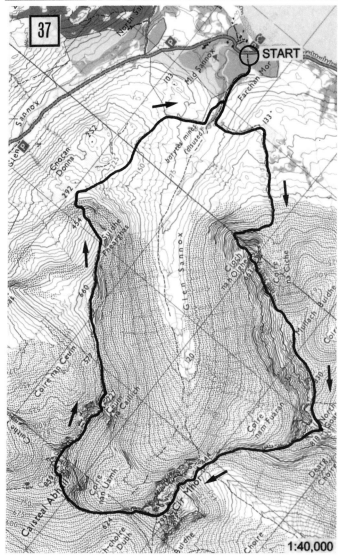

37

START

1:40,000

which includes Cioch na h'Oighe, Cir Mhor, Caisteal Abhail and Suidhe Fhearghas. The track climbs more gently, passing a small level green to the left, a footbridge and line of beech trees to the right. The ruins of old mine buildings are passed, then a rocky burn called the Allt a' Chapuill has to be forded in an area of spoil from an old barytes mine.

Turn left after fording the Allt a' Chapuill and follow a vague path upstream. The narrow path climbs up a rugged slope of grass, heather, bracken and bog myrtle. There are a series of small waterfalls in the burn, though these are sometimes obscured by birch trees which overhang the rocky gorge. When the last of the trees beside the burn are passed, the path and burn swing to the right. The path runs across a squelchy bowl of moorland, aiming more directly towards Cioch na h'Oighe. This more level stretch is followed by a steeper, bouldery, heathery slope; still with a trodden path. Again there are waterfalls along the course of the Allt a' Chapuill, and the flow seems more substantial at this point.

Don't follow the Allt a' Chapuill all the way up into Coire na Ciche, but cut off to the right across a slope of heather and boulders. The aim is to pick up the course of a narrow, gravelly path which slices across the middle slopes of Cioch na h'Oighe. The path is quite clear at close quarters, but it is difficult to spot from below, and might be missed altogether by walkers who climb too high. Follow the narrow path across the steep slope, which has no real difficulties. The path turns a corner and has a view into Glen Sannox, but it is important not to be drawn into the glen. Instead, look out for a clear, narrow path which starts zig-zagging steeply uphill to the left. This path climbs up to a sloping face of rock, and appears to terminate. Looking upwards, there appears to be a difficult scramble ahead. Retrace steps for a few paces to locate the start of an easier scramble.

The rock is bare, but there are good hand and foot holds. The path continuing uphill is rather vague in places, but it is generally possible to gauge its continuation without too much difficulty. The course of the trodden path often zig-zags and any scrambles up rocky outcrops tend to be short and fairly easy. In fact, there is nothing as difficult as the first scramble at the start of this steep climb. The path later begins to move across the slope, so that views at one point overlook Glen Sannox, then later they overlook Coire

Looking back along the rocky ridge to Caisteal Abhail

na Ciche. After the final scramble the summit of Cioch na h'Oighe is revealed as a bare hump of granite at 663m, and there are awesomely rocky views ahead around Glen Sannox.

Don't be tempted to walk off Cioch na h'Oighe in the direction of a switchback ridge, as there is overhanging rock projecting over the ridge. Instead, leave the summit of Cioch na h'Oighe as if dropping directly into Glen Sannox. A path can be joined which, by turning left, leads down to a little gap in the rollercoaster ridge. Climb uphill, following the path and a rocky scramble onto the narrow, rocky crest of the switchback ridge. Walk carefully along the ridge, cutting off to the right where the path drops down to the next gap and avoids a rockstep. Climb onto the next hump on the ridge, noting a small, creeping juniper on the way. The next two notches in the ridge are linked by a path which picks its way across the flank overlooking Glen Sannox. Both notches feature strange upstanding spikes of granite. Continue along the rocky crest, crossing the highest part of the rollercoaster ridge. Follow a well worn path across a broad gap. The path climbs up to some blocky slabs on the flanks of Mullach Buidhe, then continues up a slope littered with large, low boulders. The path easily picks a way uphill between the boulders, then there is an easier grassy slope at a higher level. A broad crest of grass and low boulders has a good path which continues all the way across Mullach Buidhe. There are a couple of jumbled rocky outcrops overlooking Glen Sannox, but a more ordered pyramidal outcrop is the highest point on Mullach Buidhe at 830m.

There is a clear view ahead around Glen Sannox and towards Goat Fell. The ridge path runs down past embedded boulders to reach a gap below North Goat Fell. There are two paths ahead. The one to the right is used to reach the summit of North Goat Fell. The steep path climbs up a grassy slope, passing rocks to reach the crest of the fell. Turn left to reach the summit of bare granite on top of North Goat Fell at 818m.

Descending from North Goat Fell to The Saddle requires care. First drop down a chaotic arrangement of boulders, then walk down to cross an exposed step. Head down some rotten ribs and grooves of granite, where there is some security to be gained from wedging the body in the grooves. A buttress ahead has a curious rocky projection on the Glen Sannox side, but pass it on the Glen Rosa side to continue downhill. There are areas of rotten granite where gritty material is strewn across the slopes. Follow a worn path onto a bouldery ridge where there are few problems. There is a short, level, easy stretch on a heathery shoulder. Pick a way along a little ledge of rock overlooking Glen Sannox, then drop down a slope of clean granite. There is rotten, crumbling granite to cross before landing on the gap of The Saddle. Ahead are the awesomely rocky slopes of Cir Mhor.

Climbing uphill from The Saddle is relatively easy at first, where slopes of heather and granite slabs are pitched at a good gradient. The slope becomes steeper and trickier, with outcropping rock, slabs, boulders and loose stones and grit. A brief, easier interlude follows along a well trodden path. Above is the final part of the ascent, which needs great care. Very steep granite proves to be rotten and worn down to a treacherously bouldery and gritty condition. The boulders are sometimes jammed in heaps or wedged in gullies, but there are some loose specimens too. The nature of this ascent is always going to be subject to change and must always be approached with extreme caution. Every hand and foot hold needs to be checked for stability. Above is the fine rock peak of Cir Mhor at 799m.

Leave by picking a way downhill carefully on rock and boulders. Look for traces of a path heading towards a gap on the way to Caisteal Abhail. The path is clearer on the final stages of the descent, crossing the gap and passing a cairn. Continue uphill, following the path along a blunt ridge and passing a couple more cairns. The top of Caisteal Abhail features a handful of blocky granite tors which have the appearance of ruined castles. On a fine day they offer a host of interesting scrambling routes. The main summit is on one of these tors, ending with a granite slab at 859m, which is easily gained and offers fine views.

Leave the summit of Caisteal Abhail by tracing a ridge path roughly eastwards. The path passes a couple of blocky tors, which adventurous walkers might like to scramble across. The path runs out onto a deceptively gentle, grassy shoulder, then drops down more ruggedly to a bouldery gap. Rising above this gap is a rocky, blocky sawtooth ridge, which is best avoided by tracing a path across the Glen Sannox flank of the ridge. Just before reaching Ceum na Caillich, or the Witch's Step, there is another bouldery tor furnishing a short scramble.

Crossing the Witch's Step calls for care and attention, a good head for heights and a willingness to use hands as well as feet. The descent into the gap is on granite slabs which fall quite steeply. Always look for signs of previous passage, and use the available hand and foot holds. Don't drop down to any place without being confident that the move can be reversed. While the broad slabs can be unnerving, there are useful steps encountered on the final few steps down into the gap. The gap is a worn, yet sharp ridge. Towering above it is a steep and blocky granite peak which walkers will be pleased to hear that they don't climb. Exit to the left of the gap, picking a way down a rather worn gully. Look to the right for a short scramble uphill, which shows obvious signs of use. A narrow path picks its way round a steep and rocky slope. There is another short scramble up some jammed boulders, then the path works its way back towards the main ridge. A moment's pause is in order at this point.

The ridge is fairly narrow as it descends, but there is a good path which cuts through the heather and crosses ribs of granite. A large boulder is passed before the next gap is reached. The path then climbs up a broader ridge featuring short grass, heather, low outcrops and boulders of granite. There is a minor summit to cross, followed by a little gap, then a worn and gritty path runs uphill onto Suidhe Fhearghas. This point is mostly rock with a little short grass and heather. There is a pointed block projecting over Glen Sannox which makes the summit more easily identified in mist. The altitude is 660m and views take in the whole of Glen Sannox, with Beinn a' Chliabhain filling the deep gap of The Saddle.

The path runs plainly down the ridge in a series of giant steps separated by short level stretches. There are low outcrops and boulders amid the grass and heather, while areas of rotting granite make the path rather gritty. Towards the end of the ridge there is a spread of gritty ground followed by a broad, low outcrop of granite. Beyond that point there is a sudden steepening towards Sannox. The path swings to the left and runs steep and stony down a rugged slope. Note that there is a slab of rock to be crossed towards the foot of the slope. This can be avoided by taking action well in advance. Look out for a rowan tree in a gully and cut off to the left well above it, following a vague path which introduces a loop into the descent. This loop later swings right and runs beneath the slab.

There is a broad, boggy, heathery gap at the foot of this slope, where paths can be distinguished heading to left and right. The path to the right is fairly clear and it cuts across the heathery gap towards Glen Sannox. Follow the path down slopes of heather, crossing patches of bracken, to reach the lower grass and bracken slopes. Note the spoils of the old barytes mines and aim for the top of these. A broad mine incline track can be followed down towards the river. Turn left around the corner of a tall deer fence, walking along a path through the bracken between the fence and the river. Cross over a wide wooden bridge and walk up to a track beside a stand of beech trees. Turn left to follow the track out of Glen Sannox, retracing the earliest steps of the day to reach the main road beside Glen Cottage.

WALK 38
Corrie & Goat Fell

There is a rugged, entertaining horseshoe route which climbs high above the villages of Sannox and Corrie. It embraces the summits of Cioch na h'Oighe, Mullach Buidhe, North Goat Fell and Goat Fell. The initial climb involves short rock scrambles and there is also an airy rock ridge to be followed. The route is not recommended in wintry or windy conditions, and in mist care is needed with navigation. There are easy escapes from the higher parts of the route, but on the ascent of Cioch na h'Oighe it is necessary to stick strictly to the route described. Short-cutting is asking for trouble and early descents are inadvisable before Mullach Buidhe. In clear weather, there is a chance to get to grips with the granite and enjoy amazing views into the rocky heart of northern Arran. The route described ends with a short road walk between Corrie and Sannox. This could be completed at the start of the walk, the end of the walk, or omitted entirely by catching a convenient bus between the two villages.

The Route

Distance:	9¹/₂ miles (15km)
Start:	Glen Cottage, Sannox, grid ref 016454.
Terrain:	Mostly on well trodden paths, but some exposed scrambling on rock in places.

Start in between Sannox and Sannox Bridge, where there is roadside parking available near a riverside toilet block. Directly opposite the car park is Glen Cottage and a sign indicates the start of the cart track into Glen Sannox. Go through a tall gate and follow the narrow tarmac track uphill. It seems to head directly for Cioch na h'Oighe, but quickly bends to the right at a series of small graveyards. The track is rough and cobbly as it continues uphill and there is another tall gate to pass through. Tall white coastal marker posts stand either side of the track, then there is a fine view around Glen Sannox which includes Cioch na h'Oighe, Cir Mhor, The Pinnacles and Suidhe Fhearghas. The track climbs more gently, passing a small

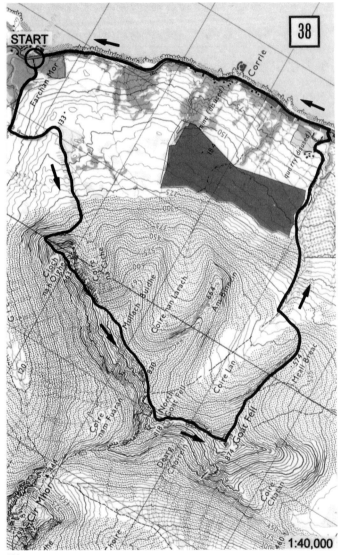

level green to the left, a footbridge and line of beech trees to the right. The ruins of old mine buildings are passed, then a rocky burn called the Allt a' Chapuill has to be forded in an area of spoil from an old barytes mine.

Turn left after fording the Allt a' Chapuill and follow a vague path upstream. The narrow path climbs up a rugged slope of grass, heather, bracken and bog myrtle. There are a series of small waterfalls in the burn, though these are sometimes obscured by birch trees which overhang the rocky gorge. When the last of the trees beside the burn are passed, the path and burn swing to the right. The path runs across a squelchy bowl of moorland, aiming more directly towards Cioch na h'Oighe. This more level stretch is followed by a steeper, bouldery, heathery slope; still with a trodden path. Again there are waterfalls along the course of the Allt a' Chapuill, and the flow seems more substantial at this point.

Don't follow the Allt a' Chapuill all the way up into Coire na Ciche, but cut off to the right across a slope of heather and boulders. The aim is to pick up the course of a narrow, gravelly path which slices across the middle slopes of Cioch na h'Oighe. The path is quite clear at close quarters, but it is difficult to spot from below, and might be missed altogether by walkers who climb too high. Follow the narrow path across the steep slope, which has no real difficulties. The path turns a corner and has a view into Glen Sannox, but it is important not to be drawn into the glen. Instead, look out for a clear, narrow path which starts zig-zagging steeply uphill to the left. This path climbs up to a sloping face of rock, and appears to terminate. Looking upwards, there appears to be a difficult scramble ahead. Retrace steps for a few paces to locate the start of an easier scramble.

The rock is bare, but there are good hand and foot holds. The path continuing uphill is rather vague in places, but it is generally possible to gauge its continuation without too much difficulty. The course of the trodden path often zig-zags and any scrambles up rocky outcrops tend to be short and fairly easy. In fact, there is nothing as difficult as the first scramble at the start of this steep climb. The path later begins to move across the slope, so that views at one point overlook Glen Sannox, then later they overlook Coire na Ciche. After the final scramble the summit of Cioch na h'Oighe is revealed as a bare hump of granite at 663m, and there are

A lone walker strides the switchback ridge near Cioch na h'Oighe

awesomely rocky views ahead around Glen Sannox.

Don't be tempted to walk off Cioch na h'Oighe in the direction of a switchback ridge, as there is overhanging rock projecting over the ridge. Instead, leave the summit of Cioch na h'Oighe as if dropping directly into Glen Sannox. A path can be joined which, by turning left, leads down to a little gap in the roller-coaster ridge. Climb uphill, following the path and a rocky scramble onto the narrow, rocky crest of the switchback ridge. Walk carefully along the ridge, cutting off to the right where the path drops down to the next gap and avoids a rockstep. Climb onto the next hump on the ridge, noting a small, creeping juniper on the way. The next two notches in the ridge are linked by a path which picks its way across the flank overlooking Glen Sannox. Both notches feature strange upstanding spikes of granite. Continue along the rocky crest, crossing the highest part of the rollercoaster ridge. Follow a well worn path across a broad gap. The path climbs up to some blocky slabs on the flanks of Mullach Buidhe, then continues up a slope littered with large, low boulders. The path easily picks a way uphill between the boulders, then there is an easier grassy slope at a higher level. A broad crest of grass and low boulders has a good path which continues all the way across Mullach Buidhe. There are a couple of jumbled rocky outcrops overlooking Glen Sannox, but a more ordered pyramidal outcrop is the highest point on Mullach Buidhe at 830m.

There is a clear view ahead around Glen Sannox and towards Goat Fell. The ridge path runs down past embedded boulders to reach a gap below North Goat Fell. There is a choice of two paths ahead. The one to the right can be used to reach the summit of North Goat Fell, while the one heading off to the left cuts from gap to gap and omits the rocky summit of North Goat Fell. The latter path is clear, free of difficulties and simply crosses a steep, grassy slope picking a way past a scattering of boulders. Note that there is also a path allowing a direct descent alongside Corrie Burn to reach the village of Corrie. Walkers wishing to reach the summit of North Goat Fell should follow a steep path up a grassy slope, passing rocks to reach the crest of the fell. Turn left to reach the summit of bare granite on top of North Goat Fell at 818m.

To leave the summit of North Goat Fell, follow the narrow, blocky ridge onwards, stepping down from the rock to gain an easy path which crosses a grassy gap. Rising above the gap is a pyramidal tor of wrinkled granite, on the Stacach Ridge, where three options are available. One route is an almost direct ascent, to the left of some large, jammed boulders. A less direct route uses giant steps to the right of the boulders. Both these options are exposed scrambles. Walkers can head around the base of the pyramid on the left side, overlooking the sea. Anyone climbing over the top of the tor will need to scramble down the other side. There are a couple more rocky bosses to scramble over if required. Anyone on the lower path can bypass all the rocky parts of the ridge by staying always on the seaward side of the ridge. The last ridge is mostly a jumble of boulders through which the path picks its way to the summit of Goat Fell. The top of Goat Fell is a table of granite bearing a few large boulders, a trig point and a view indicator has been provided by the Rotary Club of Kilwinning. Goat Fell is the highest summit on the Isle of Arran at 874m.

To leave the summit, follow the ridge path eastwards. The ground is bouldery, and the path reaches an outcrop of rock. Head either left or right and follow the path downhill to one side or the other of the outcrop of rock, then continue further down the bouldery ridge. The path is braided in parts and could be confusing in mist. The path reaches a more level shoulder on Meall Breac, where the main path to Brodick heads off to the right. However, keep straight on along the broad and bouldery crest, then descend a bouldery, heathery slope, where the path can be patchy in places and a couple of steps down can require the use of hands. Watch for the path drifting off to the left, down towards Corrie Burn.

The rough path fords Corrie Burn, which is quite bouldery and should present no problems except in times of severe flooding. Continue along the path, which has been restored in places as a counter-erosion measure. The path leads down to a step stile over a tall deer fence. The continuation downhill is rather rough and bouldery in places. There is a tall gate in another deer fence, then the path runs downhill not far from a stand of forestry. A clear track is joined and by turning left the route can be continued downhill, passing a small covered reservoir. A narrow tarmac road runs down to the main coastal road on the outskirts of Corrie. Turn left to walk through Corrie along the main road.

There may be a chance to obtain food or drink in the village, or wait for a bus in either direction. Walkers who wish to return to Sannox should walk all the way through Corrie, passing a bouldery and rocky shoreline with three small harbours. The long and straggly village ends with a huge boulder to the right of the road. The coastal road features only occasional glimpses of the sea as it is quite well wooded. There is a rugged, wooded cliff to the left, and a wooded raised beach to the right. Walking off the road proves to be very difficult and is not recommended. There is another huge boulder, this time to the left of the road, then after passing an outcrop of rough conglomerate rock, the village of Sannox is entered. Follow the road straight through to return to the small car park opposite Glen Cottage, where the walk started.

Corrie

A runrig farm was recorded in Corrie in 1449, and by 1773 it was divided into three farms. In addition to farming there were quarries above the village, providing cut stone and lime. There was some decline in the population during the clearances around 1830, but there were enough people remaining for churches and a school to be built. The Free Church dates from 1848, the school was provided by the eleventh Duke of Hamilton in 1870 and the Parish Church dates from 1886. There was once a Congregational Church too. Corrie has a number of features and facilities which, listed from south to north include: Corrie and Sannox Village Hall, car park, harbour and toilets, Free Church of Scotland, cycle hire, North High Corrie Croft Bunk House, Corrie Stores and post office, craft shops and the Corrie Hotel. Further on is another harbour with a war memorial, yet another harbour, Church of Scotland, Corrie Primary School and Blackrock Guest House.

WALK 39

Glen Rosa & Beinn Tarsuinn

There is an interesting little horseshoe circuit around Coire a' Bhradain on the western side of Glen Rosa. It could be completed as a circuit in its own right, or it could be used by walkers who set out on the Glen Rosa Horseshoe walk and realise that they are not going to be able to complete the full round. Beinn Nuis, Beinn Tarsuinn and Beinn a' Chliabhain form the "nails" in the horseshoe, and there is also an impressive traverse around the head of Coire Daingean included. A couple of stretches of the Garbh Allt have been surrounded by tall deer fences to prevent sheep and deer from grazing. The intention is to enable the scanty tree cover beside the burn to regenerate. The course of the path has been facilitated with tall swinging gates.

The Route

Distance:	9$^{1/2}$ miles (15km)
Start:	Glen Rosa Campsite, grid ref 002376.
Terrain:	Rough mountain walking, with some clear paths on boggy or rocky ground.

Start from the Glen Rosa Campsite. To reach the campsite from

187

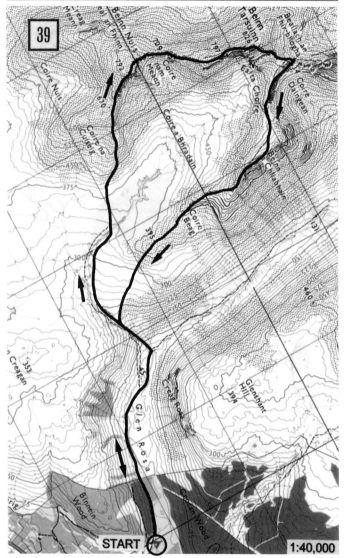

Brodick, follow the main coastal road out of town, then turn left along the Blackwaterfoot road. Turn right almost immediately along the narrow minor road signposted as the cart track for Glen Rosa. The narrow road runs past a few houses and farms, then the tarmac expires at the riverside campsite. Parking is extremely limited and taking a car as far as the campsite should be avoided if at all possible.

The cart track proceeds from the end of the road at the Glen Rosa Campsite, going through two gates and having a wood to the left at first. After passing through the second gate, the cart track runs across the open floor of Glen Rosa. The track rises and falls, twists and turns, but is generally firm, stony and dry underfoot. A point is reached where a rusty pipe spans the river and a path heads off to the left. A small sign reads: "This path has become dangerous. Please cross bridge and use path on north side of burn." Cross the footbridge and admire the waterfalls tumbling down the Garbh Allt. There are also fine views of the pyramidal peak of Cir Mhor which dominates the head of Glen Rosa, and the pinnacles either side of Ceum na Caillich - the Witch's Step - which are actually over in neighbouring Glen Sannox.

After crossing the footbridge, turn left and pick up the path which runs uphill roughly parallel to the waters of the Garbh Allt. Patches of bog myrtle near the bridge give way to bracken and heather cover as height is gained on the steep and bouldery slope. A fenced enclosure is entered at a swing gate, then the path climbs uphill. The path is rather rough, but offers better walking than the tussocks of grass alongside. There are many small waterfalls in the Garbh Allt and a small dam might be noticed where water was once collected and piped down through Glen Rosa. Another swing gate is passed and the path continues beside the burn. The waterfalls often roar down rocky slopes, while at a higher level the path runs across a gentler moorland shoulder and the river runs through a small rocky gorge. Go through a swing gate to enter another fenced enclosure surrounding the gorge. There are views around the fine little horseshoe of peaks encircling Coire a' Bhradain. Look out for a narrow little path crossing the gorge and fording the burn. A small cairn sits on the far side of the gorge to confirm the crossing point. In very wet weather it might be inadvisable to cross. Another swing gate allows an exit from the fenced enclosure, then the path climbs towards mountains.

Study the rocky ridge ahead, which features the pyramidal form of Beinn Nuis to the left, followed by Beinn Tarsuinn in the middle and Beinn a' Chliabhain to the far right. The summit of Goat Fell, which has been visible throughout the ascent, remains in view over a shoulder of Beinn a' Chliabhain. The path heads away from the burn and crosses a soggy moorland slope before steepening. After passing small slabs of granite, the path drifts to the right and follows a rib of granite. The way uphill is usually clearly trodden, except where the route crosses slabs of granite. These outcrops are set at an easy angle, but in mist it could be difficult to pick up the line of the path again afterwards. Looking across the gap between Beinn Tarsuinn and Beinn a' Chliabhain, the peaks of A' Chir and Cir Mhor can be seen.

There is a less rocky shoulder to climb before the summit of Beinn Nuis is reached. The path is very clear and as the grass and heather is much shorter the ground is quite dry. The path threads its way past low, rounded tors and boulders, before a final pull up to the summit of Beinn Nuis. Large boulders of granite protrude from the 792m summit and there is a small cairn. Views encompass Glen Rosa, with a peep through to Glen Sannox over the gap of The Saddle. Southern Arran is well displayed, but has few significant features. The Pirnmill Hills rise in a mountain barrier beyond Loch Tanna.

A path descends from the summit of Beinn Nuis, picking its way down a steep and bouldery slope before continuing along the high ridge. There are fine views of rocky buttresses overlooking Glen Rosa, then the path runs along the side of the ridge overlooking Glen Iorsa to avoid a bouldery scramble. On the next uphill stretch there is a tremendous view along the length of Glen Iorsa, featuring its little loch towards the sea, its awesomely boggy stretches along its floor, and the meandering course of its river. Walking uphill, there are many large, rounded, boulders to be passed. The ridge broadens and is clothed in short grass and moss, then it narrows and rises again. Just before a dip in the ridge the Old Man of Tarsuinn presents a sort of human profile off to the right. Cross the dip and climb a final, short, bouldery slope to reach the summit of Beinn

Tarsuinn at 826m. There are twin summits with no real difference between them; each having low outcrops and boulders of granite. Views tend to make A' Chir seem merged into Cir Mhor, but it is important to remember that these two peaks are quite separate and that there is no walker's route from one to the other.

A path runs steeply downhill from Beinn Tarsuinn to Beallach an Fhir-bhogha. There is a need to grapple with some big boulders and outcrops of granite. Sometimes there is a choice of paths, and at one point there is even the option of walking beneath a huge boulder. After much squeezing and slithering the bottom of the slope is reached and the gap of Beallach an Fhir-bhogha is gained. From certain points on the gap it is possible to see the pyramidal form of Ailsa Craig and the humps of the Paps of Jura, both out to sea in the distance, but in opposite directions.

To leave Beallach an Fhir-bhogha, turn sharply to the right to spot a path which contours beneath a monstrous granite face overlooking Coire Daingean and Glen Rosa. The path is narrow and clings to a steep slope, but it is continuous throughout. Looking upwards, tottering blocks of granite can be seen, and there is a long, dark slit slicing through the rock face. The path runs downhill on a crumbly slope, then rises to gain the crest of the ridge between Beinn Tarsuinn and Beinn a' Chliabhain. Throughout the traverse, there are fine views into Glen Rosa.

Turn left along the rocky crest, following a path which soon crosses a gentle, grassy gap. Note that the path proceeds by cutting across the western slopes of Beinn a' Chliabhain. If a summit bid is to be made, then it is necessary to start climbing to the left to stay on the ridge. Grass, heather and boulders give way to a fine rocky ridge. The summit of Beinn a' Chliabhain rises to 653m and offers fine views around Glen Rosa from an airy perch. There is a last chance to sample the distant views too, which stretch from Antrim to Galloway and Ayrshire and include Ailsa Craig and Holy Isle.

Continue along the ridge path, which joins the path skirting along the flank of the mountain. The path is clear and stony, braided in places, running down a broadening, bouldery, moorland slope. The gradient eases later, where boggy ground and granite slabs are followed by a bouldery cairn. Continue to trace the path downhill, though it is rather less clear on the broad, boggy slopes of tussocky

The Old Man of Tarsuinn gazes steadily across Glen Rosa

grass. The path swings to the left as it approaches the Garbh Allt, and it reaches a swing gate at the corner of a fenced enclosure.

All that remains is to retrace the earlier steps of the day. Follow the steep and rugged path downhill alongside the waterfalls of the Garbh Allt and pass through another swing gate at the bottom of the fenced enclosure. Turn right to cross the footbridge over the Garbh Allt, then follow the clear track through Glen Rosa to return to the campsite.

Old Man of Tarsuinn

The Old Man of Tarsuinn is a comical natural sculpture projecting from the ridge between Beinn Nuis and Beinn Tarsuinn. Its profile resembles that of Popeye, or some other gnarled seafarer, and appropriately the figure appears to gaze out to sea. After a couple of visits, walkers should be able to spot the Old Man even from distant Brodick, even though it is a mere pimple on the rocky ridge.

WALK 40

Western Glen Rosa

Tough walkers who were prepared to start early and finish late on a good, clear day would just about be able to manage the long walk around the Glen Rosa Horseshoe. Other walkers will need to tackle the round in two halves. The western half is the toughest, requiring a long ascent, some steep and rugged slopes, and even some scrambling on steep rock at times. The wrinkly rock faces of A' Chir are beyond the capabilities of more cautious walkers, and it is true that the full traverse of the rocky ridge is really the domain of rock climbers. Walkers who wish to bring the summit of A' Chir underfoot should refer to the separate short route description at the end of this section. There is a campsite on the way into Glen Rosa, and staying there in a tent gives walkers a head start on this route. Those who drive into the glen could have difficulty securing a parking space and bus services do not cover the dead-end minor road. There are many walkers prepared to cover the road-walk from Brodick to Glen Rosa, though this costs extra in terms of time, distance and effort. A taxi ride into the glen seems to be a good option, though it would be unwise to state a time for collection at the end of the day's walk. Wait and see how things progress first!

The Route

Distance:	12 miles (19km)
Start:	Glen Rosa Campsite, grid ref 002376.
Terrain:	Rough mountain walking, with some clear paths on boggy or rocky ground. Some rock scrambling is required in places.

Start from the Glen Rosa Campsite. To reach the campsite from Brodick, follow the main coastal road out of town, then turn left along the Blackwaterfoot road. Turn right almost immediately along the narrow minor road signposted as the cart track for Glen Rosa. The narrow road runs past a few houses and farms, then the tarmac expires at the riverside campsite. Parking is extremely

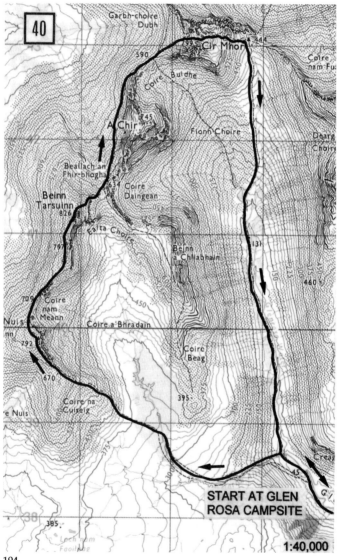

limited and taking a car as far as the campsite should be avoided if at all possible.

The cart track proceeds from the end of the road at the Glen Rosa Campsite, going through two gates and having a wood to the left at first. After passing through the second gate, the cart track runs across the open floor of Glen Rosa. The track rises and falls, twists and turns, but is generally firm, stony and dry underfoot. A point is reached where a rusty pipe spans the river and a path heads off to the left. A small sign reads: "This path has become dangerous. Please cross bridge and use path on north side of burn." Cross the footbridge and admire the waterfalls tumbling down the Garbh Allt. There are also fine views of the pyramidal peak of Cir Mhor which dominates the head of Glen Rosa, and the pinnacles either side of Ceum na Caillich - The Witch's Step - which are actually over in neighbouring Glen Sannox.

After crossing the footbridge, turn left and pick up the path which runs uphill roughly parallel to the waters of the Garbh Allt. Patches of bog myrtle near the bridge give way to bracken and heather cover as height is gained on the steep and bouldery slope. A fenced enclosure is entered at a swing gate, then the path climbs uphill. The path is rather rough, but offers better walking than the tussocks of grass alongside. There are many small waterfalls in the Garbh Allt and a small dam might be noticed where water was once collected and piped down through Glen Rosa. Another swing gate is passed and the path continues beside the burn. The waterfalls often roar down rocky slopes, while at a higher level the path runs across a gentler moorland shoulder and the river runs through a small rocky gorge. Go through a swing gate to enter another fenced enclosure surrounding the gorge. There are views around a fine little horseshoe of peaks encircling Coire a' Bhradain - the subject of a separate description (Walk 39). Look out for a narrow little path crossing the gorge and fording the burn. A small cairn sits on the far side of the gorge to confirm the crossing point. In very wet weather it might be inadvisable to cross. Another swing gate allows an exit from the fenced enclosure, then the path climbs towards mountains.

Study the rocky ridge ahead, which features the pyramidal form of Beinn Nuis to the left, followed by Beinn Tarsuinn in the middle and Beinn a' Chliabhain to the far right. The summit of Goat Fell, which has been visible throughout the ascent, remains in view over a shoulder of Beinn a' Chliabhain. The path heads away from the burn and crosses a soggy moorland slope before steepening. After passing small slabs of granite, the path drifts to the right and follows a rib of granite. The way uphill is usually clearly trodden, except where the route crosses slabs of granite. These outcrops are set at an easy angle, but in mist it could be difficult to pick up the line of the path again afterwards. Looking across the gap between Beinn Tarsuinn and Beinn a' Chliabhain, the peaks of A' Chir and Cir Mhor can be seen.

There is a less rocky shoulder to climb before the summit of Beinn Nuis is reached. The path is very clear and as the grass and heather is much shorter the ground is quite dry. The path threads its way past low, rounded tors and boulders, before a final pull up to the summit of Beinn Nuis. Large boulders of granite protrude from the 792m summit and there is a small cairn. Views encompass Glen Rosa, with a peep through to Glen Sannox over the gap of The Saddle. Southern Arran is well displayed, but has few significant features. The Pirnmill Hills rise in a mountain barrier beyond Loch Tanna.

A path descends from the summit of Beinn Nuis, picking its way down a steep and bouldery slope before continuing along the high ridge. There are fine views of rocky buttresses overlooking Glen Rosa, then the path runs along the side of the ridge overlooking Glen Iorsa to avoid a bouldery scramble. On the next uphill stretch there is a tremendous view along the length of Glen Iorsa, featuring its little loch towards the sea, its awesomely boggy stretches along its floor, and the meandering course of its river. Walking uphill, there are many large, rounded, boulders to be passed. The ridge broadens and is clothed in short grass and moss, then it narrows and rises again. Just before a dip in the ridge the Old Man of Tarsuinn presents a sort of human profile off to the right. Cross the dip and climb a final, short, bouldery slope to reach the summit of Beinn Tarsuinn at 826m. There are twin summits with no real difference between them; each having low outcrops and boulders of granite. Views tend to make A' Chir seem merged into Cir Mhor, but it is important to remember that these two peaks are quite separate and that there is no walker's route from one to the other.

The pinnacles on Cir Mhor catch the late evening sun

A path runs steeply downhill from Beinn Tarsuinn to Beallach an Fhir-bhogha. There is a need to grapple with some big boulders and outcrops of granite. Sometimes there is a choice of paths, and at one point there is even the option of walking beneath a huge boulder. After much squeezing and slithering the bottom of the slope is reached and the gap of Beallach an Fhir-bhogha is gained. From certain points on the gap it is possible to see the pyramidal form of Ailsa Craig and the humps of the Paps of Jura, both out to sea in the distance, but in opposite directions. There are two paths leaving Beallach an Fhir-bhogha; a high and low level path. The high level path heads for the summit of A' Chir and walkers are referred to a separate route for details (see end of section). Use the lower path to continue with this particular walk, which avoids the difficulties of the rocky A' Chir ridge.

The lower path leads beneath the boilerplate slabs which flank A' Chir on the Glen Iorsa side. The path is faint in places, although it should always be distinguishable ahead. It dips downhill to pass beneath the foot of the slabs. This is something of a "weeping wall" with clean granite slabs dripping or running with water, with only a few rugs or carpets of heather able to keep hold on the steep rock. The path rises from the base of the slabs and reaches a little notch in the ridge offering a view back along the more difficult parts of the A' Chir ridge. The path continues away from the summit in the direction of Cir Mhor. There is a short rockstep giving access to an inclined table of rock on the rugged crest of the ridge. The path runs down to a broad, bouldery gap, where a small cairn sits on the lowest part. Note that there is a path exiting to the right, down into Coire Buidhe, if an ascent of Cir Mhor is not required on this particular outing.

The path climbing Cir Mhor starts by wriggling up a bouldery slope. At one point there is a short link to the left with the ridge path serving Castail Abhail. Be careful not to be drawn along the ridge to Caisteal Abhail in mist. The final part of Cir Mhor rises even more steeply and the summit peak of rock is gained only by grappling with the last rocky rise. From the 799m stance there are amazing views around the ridges of Glen Rosa and Glen Sannox. The peaks of Goat Fell, Cioch na h'Oighe and Caisteal Abhail all feature prominently, as well as the A' Chir ridge which was so recently outflanked. The more distant Pirnmill Hills are seen across Glen Iorsa.

The descent from Cir Mhor to The Saddle needs exceptional care. Looking down from the summit, only a couple of portions of the path near the top can be seen. What is not apparent is the nature of the terrain. Very steep granite proves to be rotten and worn down to a treacherously bouldery and gritty condition. The boulders are sometimes jammed in heaps or wedged in gullies, but there are some loose specimens too. The nature of this descent is always going to be subject to change and must always be approached with extreme caution. The first part of the descent is steep and horrible, with every hand and foot hold needing to be checked for stability, then there is a brief easy interlude along a well trodden path. Another steep and rugged drop picks a way down a steep slope where there is outcropping rock, slabs, boulders and loose stones and grit. This steep and tricky slope continues all the way down to The Saddle. Only on the final parts of the descent are there any easy gradients, where slopes of heather and slabs pitched at an easier angle lead onto the gap.

Walkers who start to venture down towards The Saddle and suddenly find themselves backing out in fear can try an alternative descent towards Glen Rosa. Retrace steps over the top of Cir Mhor and down to the gap between Cir Mhor and A' Chir. The start of the path down to Coire Buidhe is marked by a small cairn. The first part of the path consists of steep, loose, stony material. Later, there is a gentler path, before another drop leads down through Fionn Choire into Glen Rosa.

The descent from the granite slabs of The Saddle into Glen Rosa lies along a path to the right, with a cairn helping to confirm the route. The path descends at a reasonable gradient, though it is rather worn and braided in places. Looking to the right, there is a fine view of the intricacies of the A' Chir ridge, should a traverse along it ever be contemplated. Cir Mhor completely dominates to the far right. Continue down the bouldery, heathery tongue, following the clearest path and fording a small burn. In wet weather, this could result in wet feet. Follow the path through another bouldery, heathery area at a gentler gradient, then drift towards the course of Glenrosa Water. The river is often observed sliding across slabs of granite as it drains through the glen.

Keep to the riverside path, but note that the path later moves away from the river. It has been partially restored and most of the time the surface is firm and dry. The ground to either side of the path is usually wet and boggy. The path later returns to follow the river downstream and passes a large boulder of granite. Look out for an attractive waterfall which plunges into a deep pool in a rocky gorge overhung by birch trees. The path again moves away from Glenrosa Water and crosses the footbridge over the Garbh Allt which was crossed earlier in the day. From this point, it is simply a matter of picking up the cart track and following it back towards the campsite on the way out of Glen Rosa.

Glen Rosa

Facilities in Glen Rosa are limited to the Glen Rosa Campsite and a self-catering cottage. There is also a taxi and minibus service based in the glen, for groups or individuals who wish to be able to travel in and out of the place with greater ease. Practically all of the Glen Rosa Horseshoe, and some land outside its bounds, is owned and managed by the National Trust for Scotland. The extent of their holdings is around 7000 acres.

A' Chir

Those walkers who wish to include the summit of A' Chir in this walk should note that there is some steep and exposed scrambling even on the easiest ascent. Starting from Beallach an Fhir-bhogha, take the path running uphill. This stays on the Glen Iorsa side of the rugged ridge, then gains the crest of the ridge at a notch overlooked by a monstrous buttress of rock. Take a path to the left, then scramble up boulders and slabs. Another path at a higher level picks its way along a narrow ledge on a sloping boilerplate slab overlooking Glen Iorsa, then it gains the rocky crest and reaches another notch. It is possible to scramble down into the notch in a couple of places, but the rock can be damp and greasy, and a slip could have disastrous consequences. This awkward descent can be avoided by backtracking a little along the ridge, then dropping down to another thin path on the Glen Iorsa side. The path leads along a ledge which runs into a gully just below the notch. To the left of this gully is an exposed rock scramble on sloping slabs, allowing the crest to be regained. Once this has been accomplished, walk and scramble towards the summit of A' Chir, which is a monstrous perched boulder at 745m. Walkers may be excused for not tackling this final obstacle!

Continuing along the A' Chir ridge towards Cir Mhor is fraught with difficulties and is actually graded as a rock climb. Anyone experiencing hardship scrambling to the summit of A' Chir would not be able to cover the rest of the ridge. While experienced rock climbers would be able to progress without the use of a rope, others should consider roping up for safety. A couple of experienced rock climbers using ropes might be able to get a couple more less accomplished climbers along the rest of the ridge. Cautious explorers who have managed to reach the summit of A' Chir, but don't want to be drawn along the rest of the ridge should retrace steps faithfully to Beallach an Fhir-bhogha. If anything, the descent is rather trickier than the ascent and it certainly needs more care. The first full traverse of the A' Chir ridge was accomplished in January 1892.

WALK 41
Eastern Glen Rosa

The Glen Rosa Horseshoe can be completed in a good, long, hard day's walk by tough and experienced hill walkers. Other walkers may prefer to tread more cautiously and complete the horseshoe walk in two easier halves. Note the use of the word "easier" and not "easy". The Glen Rosa Horseshoe can never be easy and there are some very steep and exposed rocky slopes. Some basic scrambling is required in places. The western half of the horseshoe has some of the more arduous scrambles, while the eastern half is somewhat easier on the hands. The walk includes Goat Fell, which is the highest mountain on the Isle of Arran and offers the most extensive views. While the eastern half of the Glen Rosa Horseshoe can be conveniently started at the Glen Rosa Campsite, there is no transport along the dead-end road and parking for cars can be tight. A taxi ride from Brodick is perhaps the best option to consider, although walkers who are prepared to camp in Glen Rosa can please themselves how and when to start the walk. Returning directly from Goat Fell to Glen Rosa at the end of the day can be difficult, so the route given to close the circuit is, although long, much easier. An alternative finish could be made at Brodick Castle or down on the main road nearby, if a handy lift can be arranged.

The Route

Distance:	11 miles (18km)
Start:	Glen Rosa Campsite, grid ref 002376.
Terrain:	Rugged paths throughout the ascent, with some short rocky scrambles. Easier road walking at the end.

Start from the Glen Rosa Campsite. To reach the campsite from Brodick, follow the main coastal road out of town, then turn left along the Blackwaterfoot road. Turn right almost immediately along the narrow minor road signposted as the cart track for Glen Rosa. The narrow road runs past a few houses and farms, then the tarmac expires at the riverside campsite. Parking is extremely

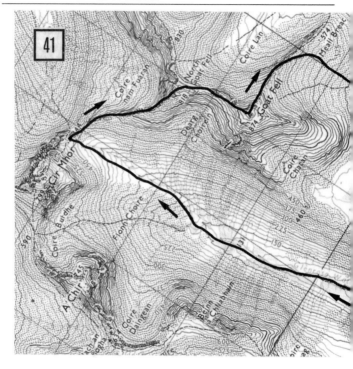

limited and taking a car as far as the campsite should be avoided if at all possible.

The cart track proceeds from the end of the road at the Glen Rosa Campsite, going through two gates and having a wood to the left at first. After passing through the second gate, the cart track runs across the open floor of Glen Rosa. The track rises and falls, twists and turns, but is generally firm, stony and dry underfoot. Cross the footbridge and admire the waterfalls tumbling down the Garbh Allt. There are also fine views of the pyramidal peak of Cir Mhor which dominates the head of Glen Rosa, and the pinnacles either side of Ceum na Caillich - the Witch's Step - which are actually over in neighbouring Glen Sannox.

A restored path leads away from the footbridge, running through

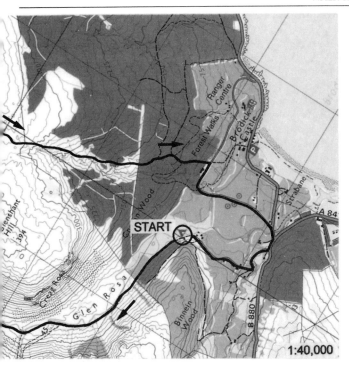

START

1:40,000

Glen Rosa. The path drifts towards Glenrosa Water, running close to an attractive waterfall which plunges into a deep pool in a rocky gorge overhung by birch trees. There is later a large granite boulder to the right of the path, which is clean and hard on all sides. Just beyond, on the left of the path, is another granite boulder which is rotten and crumbly. Both types of granite will be seen during the day's walk. The path later drifts away from the river and continues up through the boggy, bouldery glen. The surface is generally easy and dry. By the time the path returns to the riverside the water slides over slabs of granite. The path ascends through a bouldery, heathery area and there is a small burn to be forded; which could mean wet feet in wet weather.

Continue up the clearest path, climbing up a broad and bouldery tongue towards The Saddle, which is the lowest gap in the mountains ahead, between Cir Mhor to the left and North Goat Fell to the right. To the far left on the ascent there is a chance to study the intricacies of the A' Chir ridge, should a visit to that summit ever be planned. The path climbs uphill at a reasonable gradient and it is rather worn and braided in places. The path lands on The Saddle amid low outcrops of granite, with a fine view over into Glen Sannox. To the left is a very steep and rugged path leading up to the summit of Cir Mhor. To the right is the path climbing to the summit of North Goat Fell. Turning right leads across the lowest part of The Saddle, which is strewn with grit and gravel.

Clean, hard granite gives way to rotten, crumbling granite as the ridge is followed above The Saddle. More clean granite follows and there are splendid views back towards the awesomely rugged peak of Cir Mhor. There is one point where it is necessary to pick a way across a little ledge of rock overlooking Glen Sannox. Beyond is a short, level, easy stretch on a heathery shoulder. The path then climbs uphill on a bouldery ridge with no real difficulties for a while. On a higher part of the ridge there is a worn path on a grassy slope, then more rock becomes apparent towards the top. The rock is rotten and gritty material has been washed down towards Glen Rosa. There is a buttress ahead which has a curious rocky projection on the Glen Sannox side. Pass the buttress on the Glen Rosa side and regain the crest of the ridge at a notch. Ribs and grooves of granite, although rotten, offer some security on an uphill scramble. There is an exposed step to negotiate before the next uphill pull. The final climb crosses a chaotic arrangement of boulders and reaches an inclined slab which is the summit of North Goat Fell at 818m.

To leave the summit of North Goat Fell, follow the narrow, blocky ridge onwards, stepping down from the rock to gain an easy path which crosses a grassy gap to the right. Rising above the gap is a pyramidal tor of wrinkled granite, on the Stacach Ridge, where three options are available. One route is an almost direct ascent, to the left of some large, jammed boulders. A less direct route uses giant steps to the right of the boulders. Both these options are exposed scrambles. Walkers can head around the base of the pyramid on the left side, overlooking the sea. Anyone climbing over the top of the tor will need to scramble down the other side. There are a couple more rocky bosses to scramble over if required. Anyone on the lower path can bypass all the rocky parts of the ridge by staying always on the seaward side of the ridge. The last ridge is mostly a jumble of boulders through which the path picks its way to the summit of Goat Fell. The top of Goat Fell is a table of granite bearing a few large boulders. A trig point and a view indicator has been provided by the Rotary Club of Kilwinning. Goat Fell is the highest summit on the Isle of Arran at 874m.

To leave the summit, follow the ridge path eastwards. The ground is bouldery, and the path reaches an outcrop of rock. Head either right or left of the outcrop and follow the path downhill, then continue further down the bouldery ridge. The path is braided in parts and could be confusing in mist. The path reaches a more level shoulder on Meall Breac, at which point it heads off to the right. The line of the path has been restored and features pitched stonework, drains and a gravelly surface. The surrounding moorland is mostly wet, grassy, heathery and bouldery. On some short stretches the path runs over granite slabs. A tall deer fence is reached and a gate gives access to a more rugged lower path. (Following this deer fence offers a more rugged return to Glen Rosa, ending with a river crossing.) The path runs down a heathery slope and crosses a channel of water which has been constructed across the hillside. Stands of forestry lie some distance from the path, and the heather and bracken slope features a few areas of birch.

The path goes through an old gateway in a drystone wall, then goes through a strip where rhododendron bushes have been cut back. Continue down through a crossroads of forest tracks, going straight onwards and straight downhill. At the next junction, turn right and continue downhill. Take no notice of waymarks pointing to left or right, but simply walk down the most obvious track. Looking back, some markers state that the track is leading to Goat Fell, and by the time a narrow tarmac road is reached there is a signboard bearing a map outlining the extent of the National Trust for Scotland's upland holdings on the Isle of Arran.

The road could be followed to the left to reach Brodick Castle, though it may well be closed this late in the day. The track crosses the road and could be followed straight onwards down to the Arran Craft Centre and the main road. Turning right along the road leads past the large house known as The Kennels. The road continues across a bridge in a wooded area, then runs downhill and through fields. Well trimmed beech hedges obscure a view of three tall standing stones: one to the left of the road and two to the right. The road continues to a gate lodge where there is an exit onto the main road. Turn right and cross a bridge, then right again along the Blackwaterfoot road. Another right turn is signposted for Glen Rosa, running back to the campsite where the walk started.

Glen Rosa
See Walk 40.

PRINTED BY
CARNMOR PRINT & DESIGN, LONDON RD, PRESTON, U.K.